From Banda Machines to Google Classroom

My life in teaching

By
Jon Hall

Grosvenor House
Publishing Limited

This book is published by
Grosvenor House Publishing Ltd
Link House
140 The Broadway, Tolworth, Surrey, KT6 7HT.
www.grosvenorhousepublishing.co.uk

A CIP record for this book
is available from the British Library

Paperback ISBN 978-1-83615-338-2
eBook ISBN 978-1-83615-339-9

Contents

Foreword

Perhaps I've always been planning to write this book. Maybe that's the reason I didn't throw away any of my academic diaries at the end of each school year. Over the years, the line of them in my various stock cupboards has got longer and longer. When I finally retired, there were 38 of them altogether, and they came home with me. They have been my main source for writing what follows, supplemented by the internet for the odd bit of fact checking when timelines have got a bit confused in my head.

My original plan was to write about what I was up to on the same date every year, in the style of the couple in the brilliant *One Day* by David Nicholls. It struck me fairly early on that to stick with this religiously would mean that quite a few of the 38 years would fall on weekend dates, when generally I wasn't involved in anything to do with school. (I've tried, particularly in the second half of my working life, to work long hours in the week and leave the weekends as free as possible for other activities.) So, I changed that initial idea slightly and chose various dates each year in October, when my diaries suggested a starting point for what I hope you will find is something vaguely interesting to do with the life of a late twentieth/ early twenty first century teacher. Why choose October? No particular reason really, other than it's a fairly typical teaching month- you're getting into the swing of the new academic year, you're beginning to get to know your new class(es) reasonably well and you've got a week off at the end of it to look forward to.

Acknowledgements

My thanks go to the pupils, parents, governors and staff of the three Hertfordshire schools where what follows all happened: Lyndhurst Middle School, Borehamwood (1986-1992), Fair Field Junior School, Radlett (1993-1999) and Bishop Wood CE Junior School, Tring (1999-2024.)

And also, of course, to all my friends and family for their encouragement and support over the years.

Prologue

"Welcome to Lyndhurst!"

Monday, 28th April 1986

My train pulls out of Bournemouth Station at some ungodly hour, but I've always preferred to be hours early rather than minutes late, and today is a day where being late is not really an option. I'm travelling via London to Borehamwood in Hertfordshire for an interview for my first ever teaching job. This is the sixteenth job I've applied for, and the second for which I've made the shortlist. I've picked up a few dos and don'ts from my only other interview, where I was edged out by a Cambridge undergraduate for a post in New Romney, Kent, so maybe it'll be my turn this time.

I'm almost at the end of a four-year BEd course at the Dorset Institute of Higher Education. I've absolutely loved it, but the time to face the real world is fast approaching. I've fallen in love with the county of Dorset and its motorway free world, its endearing place names (I've played cricket at Owermoigne and Melplash, for example) and its slower pace of life. The urge to be fussy and stay until I get a job in my new adopted county has been a strong one. But teaching jobs down here are hard to come by- it's such a lovely part of the world, once people are here, they tend to stay. So, I've been applying everywhere, eager to put my newfound skills to the test, to get on with life and change the world by influencing the next generation of children for the better.

Borehamwood, when I arrive bleary eyed at some point mid-morning, doesn't seem that different to my childhood home of Bexleyheath, diagonally opposite on the map if you draw a line through London, and about the same distance from the centre. They're only 30 miles or so apart as the crow flies, but I've never been here before. I wander down the High Street and come across the world-famous Elstree Studios. I had no idea that was here, but I suppose the fact the station was called Borehamwood and Elstree was a bit of a clue.

In my one and only suit, a light grey pinstripe, I present myself at the school reception desk and the whirlwind of an interview day starts again. I answer the questions of the interview panel as confidently as I can, without, I hope, appearing too much of a 'know-it-all', and sit in the staff room trying to make small talk with the teachers, who greet me warmly and feel like people I could work with happily if I'm offered the chance.

A key question nearly always asked at the end of an interview is something along the lines of, 'If we offered you the job today, would you take it?' I answer this with a resounding 'yes!' This, I find out much later, is the most important answer of the day. Apparently, the role comes down to a choice between me and one of the other candidates, who at the key moment hedges his bets between this job and an interview that he has elsewhere a few days hence.

So, I'm in. Shirley, my new boss, reaches across her immaculate desk, shakes my hand, smiles encouragingly, looks me in the eyes and says, "Welcome to Lyndhurst." My ambition to become a teacher, born five or so years previously whilst watching *To Serve them all my Days* on TV, has been realised. All I need to do now is finish those last few exams, find somewhere to live, and turn up here again in September, raring to go.

Chapter 1

"Don't smile till Christmas!"

Wednesday, 22nd October 1986

You can see it written on the faces of some of the parents "is this young whippersnapper really in charge of my child's development until next Summer?" (I'm only twenty two years old and barely ten years older than my young charges.) Today is my first Parents Evening as a teacher. I can't remember much advice about how to handle these being given on my B.Ed course, so it's in at the deep end.

But, for the most part, the parents keep this thought to themselves, and the early feedback is encouraging. Most of the kids seem to be reasonably happy in my class and it would appear, as I'd hoped, that there is a genuine rapport with at least some of them. "Don't smile till Christmas" one of my colleagues had said in the first week of term- a reference to the undoubted truth that it's much easier to relax with a class once you've established all the ground rules and got them working as you want, rather than starting out all free and easy and having to back-track when the pupils don't work or mess about or both. I've probably smiled a few times most days but the balance between Attila the Hun and Mother Teresa has been about right.

And, to my secret relief, some of the parents of the more difficult children don't turn up. Half of my blood is Northern, and I have a tendency at times to speak my mind when a more diplomatic form of words would be more prudent. I haven't yet worked out how to subtly tell someone that their child makes large parts of my working day very difficult. The catchment area of the school is a mixed one, and some of the parents aren't desperately bothered about how their offspring are doing as long as they're here and we're not hassling them.

My decision to trust to fate and apply for jobs everywhere has paid dividends. I've really landed on my feet at Lyndhurst. I enjoy working with my class and I have a supportive and fun year group team in Carole and Nikki. I've also managed to get a teacher's flat on the other side of town at a very reasonable rent.

Even better, it's half term next week so get through tonight and two more days then I can sleep for hours and hours and hours. I never knew it was possible to feel this tired. I did a whole term's teaching practice last year, but there was always the student bar in the evening when lesson plans had been done, always others who'd had a worse day than me, and we were driven there by minibus. No peddling home up a long hill with Tesco bags stuffed full of books to be marked dangling precariously from the handlebars.

Chapter 2

"I'm gonna do well well!"

Thursday, 8th October 1987

I'm not what you'd call a naturally gifted sportsman, but I love sport and have a modicum of talent in some games, so a lot of my early teaching is in PE. I'm teaching in a "Middle School" for pupils aged 9-13, and it's run to some extent on secondary lines, so that you can choose to teach subjects that interest you and that you know something about. So, PE is on my list and while specialists are teaching my class, 2H, subjects like art, metalwork and home economics, about which I know next to nothing, I am to be found on the field or in the gym teaching how to pass a rugby ball or execute a badminton drop shot.

Earlier this week, though, I've been distinctly out of my comfort zone on a course for trampolining teachers. I'm due to teach this for the first time soon, and before the LEA will let me loose on such a dangerous piece of equipment, they wisely insist on me completing a qualification of competence. The coaching side is not too bad; although I lack the co-ordination to perform seat drops, front drops and the rest with the required finesse, I can grasp the teaching points satisfactorily enough, and back at school there will always be an able child to demonstrate said manoeuvres.

No, my real problems start when I am asked to put away the trampoline and then safely get it out again. I am not technically minded and this proves very difficult. Mum tells me I am the product of a very long labour ("I thought they might have to use forceps"), and as my poor skills in this area of life have been revealed to my family over the years, speculation has increased that maybe the long labour caused some mild brain damage. Anyway, I can't crack this and the blessed thing keeps collapsing under my direction. The kindly LEA

(Local Education Authority) adviser smiles and offers a personal visit to my school to help.

Another worrying aspect of the course is highlighted when the tutor tells us an anecdote from a school in Leeds. Some teenagers apparently broke into a school there one night a couple of years ago. They got the trampoline out, started jumping up and down on it, and one of the lads fell off and broke his neck. The boy's parents successfully sued the LEA for damages, because the trampoline wasn't locked. So, if I learnt nothing else this week, it was to make sure our trampoline is always locked!

But today I am back on more familiar territory. It's the 2nd Year football team's local derby away to Holmshill, one of the other two middle schools in the town. I'm young and full of energy, so I devote most evenings after school to running one sort of sports club or another- three football teams this term have the benefit of my tactical know-how. And today I will be pitting my wits against another fresh-faced teacher, Marcus, coach of Holmshill.

Our school is strong in PE, and in just over a year, I've already seen how school sport can help keep some of the less academically inclined on-side at school. The head of PE, Yvonne, is a most impressive figure and one of a handful of colleagues whom I'm already basing my attitudes and expectations on. The quality of her gym club's displays is breathtaking and very few bring in sickness or injury notes for her lessons. Any girls who try to play the period card will not get away with it more than once a month, because she keeps a meticulous record of all excuses!

Sports Day last term was very keenly contested between the houses, and followed weeks of intense build-up in lessons and after school clubs, with enthusiasm reaching boiling point in time for the big day. The Deputy Head overheard one excited pupil blurt out "I'm gonna do well well in Sports Day!" The word 'well', I should explain, is currently the prefix of a number of other words in common usage amongst the pupils, with 'crucial' and 'wicked' being also particularly favoured.

The football is close, as I expected it would be. We shade a tight first half and are 1-0 up at the break. But then in the second half defences tire and the goals start to stream in- at both ends. Tempers become a little frayed on the touchline, and I do my best to walk the fine line between encouraging our team, and not pandering to the parents' rather warped view of how Marcus is refereeing the game. Refereeing school matches is horrendously difficult- you want your team to do well, but are paranoid about being accused of bias towards them and if anything tend to over-compensate and favour the opposition. Parents refereeing from the side and shouting their opinions do not help. I've already had to threaten to abandon one game when exuberance crossed the boundary into abuse and rather 'colourful' language. At the end of a breathless second half, we have triumphed by the odd goal in nine, and I can look forward to delivering a detailed report in assembly tomorrow.

Chapter 3

"The fees are as much as Eton!"

Thursday, 13th October 1988

I'm now in my third year of teaching and I'm feeling quite pleased with myself because already I've gained a promotion, and have started climbing the career ladder. Since last month I've been in receipt of what they're now calling an 'A' allowance- this means I get about an extra £1K per annum on top of my basic wage for doing something other teachers don't normally do.

I've been lucky really, in that a couple of senior colleagues have moved on in the last couple of years, and their roles need to be taken by other, younger teachers, and that means me! So, towards the end of last term, my Headteacher called me in, said I had impressed people with my work in the school so far, and would I like to take on the EWO liaison role? I had an inkling what that meant, but not really much of an idea exactly what the role involved. But, a promotion is a promotion, so I said yes, had a crash course in the job from the previous postholder, a chat a couple of weeks later with a Governor who had to rubber-stamp the appointment, and now here I am!

EWO stands for Education Welfare Officer, and he visits us every Thursday afternoon. He has a very interesting and varied job description. Not that long ago he might have been called a Truant Officer, and he does spend a fair bit of his time knocking on doors of children who aren't attending school enough, and trying to find out why. Another of his roles is to escort children from the local area to special boarding schools away from the area. These are children with emotional and behavioural issues of such significance that it's been decided they need to be away from family and their local environment in order to try and get them back on track. Terry never tires of telling

6

me that the LEA are paying the equivalent of the fees at Eton for one of his young clients.

My job involves two non-contact periods every week. On a Wednesday morning, I go through the registers, and note any lengthy or unaccounted for absences. I put notes in registers asking teachers to chase up things, and then anything I am concerned about I can raise in my second non-contact period the following day, when Terry, the EWO, comes calling. Sometimes this meeting is preceded by a lunchtime conflab with Tina, the School Nurse.

To say this is an eye-opener would be an understatement. Some of these children are dealing with some very difficult problems, and frankly I'm not sure if I could face school if I was trying to deal with what they're having to. Today I've got four cases I want to talk to Terry about- all boys, although that isn't necessarily typical. He answers my queries with good humour and his experience helps me sort trifling concerns from the potentially more serious. In the end, only one of the four requires immediate follow-up by him, so I will need to talk to that teacher and bring them up to date.

Nagging teachers for absence details and telling them that one of their pupils is an EWO concern is my first experience of putting potentially more work on my colleagues, and I'm finding it hard at the moment to deal with their occasional (and understandable) annoyance at this, but I guess if I don't want to remain a teaching foot-soldier for the rest of my career, this is something I will have to get used to.

It's also my first experience of dealing with parents of children whom I'm not actually teaching. If an absence goes unexplained for more than a week, I have to follow this up myself and put a call to home in. This is tricky for me because I've never been the most confident or assertive user of the telephone; already, I'm coming to dread this part of the job, and I'm never that disappointed if there's nobody at home when I call. A real bonus is if nobody is in, but they have an answer phone- then I can get my point across without actually having to speak to someone!

Chapter 4

"How are you going to eat?"

Wednesday, 18th October 1989

Last year's Education Act is starting to bite. We now have an American style all-through year numbering system, so that your first year in school is called Year R (for reception) and the Upper Sixth (if you get that far) is called Year 13. So, at Lyndhurst, we have Years 5-8, and our year groups and classes have been renamed accordingly. More importantly, we have a new 'National Curriculum' and this means there is now a lot less choice over what we can teach, and when. My colleague in Year 5 who has taught the Romans every Autumn Term more or less since the Romans left these shores just because that's what she's always done, can no longer necessarily do so. And that's probably a good thing isn't it? The Government are saying that, amongst other benefits, the more centralised curriculum will mean it will be easier for children who move from one part of the country to another. It's a step towards the French system, where apparently the Education Minister can look at the clock on the wall in his or her office at say, eleven o'clock on a Thursday morning, and pretty much know what all 8 year olds in the country will be being taught at that moment. All sounds a bit Big Brother-ish to me!

Anyway, the arrival of a National Curriculum has certainly caused a few headaches for those of us working in Middle Schools. The new curriculum has been divided into 4 'key stages.' Key Stage 1 is children aged 5-7 (ie infants)- no problem for us, as we don't have any. Key Stage 2 is children aged 7-11 (ie Juniors)- well we have some of them but so do our feeder First Schools. Key Stage 3 is children aged 11-14. Well, we have the first two years of that group, but then they move onto Upper School. So how do we decide the content of what is taught in the various years? We have a whole series of meetings with colleagues in other schools across the town, that's how. And in terms of History and Geography, that's down to me.

This is because I've quickly moved up from an 'A' allowance to a 'B' allowance and have joined the ranks of the school 'Senior Staff' team. I'm Head of Integrated Studies (that's what we call History and Geography), and a Year Leader too- responsible for the pastoral care of about 90 children. Another experienced colleague moved on last Easter, there was very little interest in the job from outside, and the Headteacher and Governors took a chance on me (again.) Whilst not exactly rolling in money, it's another welcome top-up to the salary. My partner and I joined the home-owning classes last year, and the Financial Adviser, who did nevertheless grant us the mortgage, looked up from the figures at one point and said rather worryingly, "this is all very well, but how are you going to eat?" Well the 'B' allowance is helping to keep the wolf from the door, as they say.

So, this afternoon, I'm experiencing only my third ever 'Senior Staff' meeting. These important gatherings are so important, and the attendees such an exclusive lot, that they take place not in the staff room, but in the confines of the Head's study- and it's still called that, not the Head's office. It's a room that I generally feel comfortable and positive in, as it was within these four walls that I was offered the chance to officially join the teaching profession about three and a half years ago now. Although I've learnt a lot in the interim and can hold my own in most of the discussions, I'm still slightly in awe of some of my senior colleagues, particularly the Head and the Deputy. Their jobs are tough, and yet they come back here day after day and manage, outwardly at least, to take everything in their stride.

During the last three years, I've sometimes experienced a slight feeling of jealous exclusion when I've not been able to attend these meetings. Thoughts like "what on earth are they discussing in there?" have gone through my mind. But now I'm in here, I realise it's just fairly mundane stuff, but on a slightly more 'whole school' level than general staff meetings. Today, for instance, we focus mainly on tomorrow evening's Prospective Parents Evening, and what we can do to encourage our visitors to send their offspring here next year.

So, a large part of my time from now on will be spent in meetings. National Curriculum meetings with colleagues from other schools, pastoral care meetings about children in my Year Group, Senior Staff meetings, and ordinary staff meetings. That's a lot of meetings.

Chapter 5

"No chairs if there are any more problems!"

Friday, 19th October, 1990

This year, Senior Staff at our school haven't been given our standard issue 'Education Year Diary.' We have a very trendy 'Management Handbook and Diary' instead. And it's in thick 'filofax' format, so if we take it out with us at weekends and stroll casually down the street with it, we could be mistaken for 'yuppies.'

There's space for me to write copious notes on all sorts of topics and certainly a lot of ink is being taken up due to my newfound role as Year Leader. This is a job that gives you an insight into people's lives in a way that my training and very early years of teaching did not. It is a real eye opener to me, coming as I do from a stable background and a generally happy home, what some of the 12- and 13-year-olds in my care are having to put up with.

Custody court cases, bullying, evictions, domestic abuse, substance abuse, lateness, children running out of school, parents being imprisoned and shoplifting have all come to my attention in just over a year in the job. Sometimes it's a wonder to me that these children are able to focus on their learning at all given what's going on.

I use most of my 3 free periods each week (the other 22 are spent teaching English, PE, RE and Integrated Studies) trying to keep on top of all this, liaising with parents, talking to the children and offering support and guidance where I can. But often it's just listening. I can't wave a magic wand and solve these problems, much as I'd love to. Sometimes I can pass the child or parent on to some other professional or agency that might be able to help. I lean a lot on other colleagues, particularly John, the Deputy Head, to help me with all this.

The other aspect of all this is in some respects even harder. As well as trying to help these children, I'm also responsible for their discipline and behaviour. If they're messing about in lessons, in assembly or on the playground, it's down to me to do something about it. I'm beginning to dread a colleague sidling up to me with an opening line of , "Oooh Jon, I'm glad I've caught you, I've been meaning to have a word with you about...." I've even found myself occasionally finding excuses not to go in the staff room for fear of such an encounter, and that's not a healthy place to be in.

Individual misdemeanours are best dealt with via a quiet word at a break or lunchtime, or a phone call home. But each Friday, I get a twenty-five-minute assembly with my year group, and I use this to celebrate the successes of my young charges and also appeal to their better nature if things are not going well. It's a challenge not to turn this into constant moaning about uniform transgressions and being unkind to younger pupils, but so far this term I've also managed to give a fair bit of praise for hard work and for volunteering to help with various things around the school. Today, I've written in my filofax, "No chairs if there are any more problems." I have been inundated with complaints since the start of term about Year 8's behaviour in assembly. As the top year in the school, Year 8 are allowed chairs to sit on in assembly, but I threaten to remove that privilege in a bid to get them to sit still and stay quiet. We will see how that goes.....

Chapter 6

"Conkers-holes at home, litter, not indoors!"

Thursday, 17th October 1991

The conker season is in full swing at Lyndhurst. The tradition that I enjoyed so much as a child is still alive and kicking. It features heavily in our morning briefing today, and I scribble the title of this chapter into my diary. There are three golden rules that it's been agreed we need to try and enforce with our classes: firstly, the holes in the conkers must be made at home. This means that kitchen skewers and the like will hopefully not be brought into school.

Secondly, any litter made by the playground battles (i.e. the leftover smashed up conkers) needs to be picked up and put in a bin. Finally, indoor conker fighting is expressly forbidden!

There are one or two murmurs of dissent about whether conkers should be allowed at all given the possible damage to pupils' hands and knuckles, but in the end these guidelines are generally accepted, and they seem to do the trick and, broadly speaking, the children have lots of harmless fun as a result.

However, I am noticing more discussions in school around the Health and Safety of our pupils. Perhaps it's just because I'm now a member of the Senior Staff team and more tuned into these matters than I was at the start of my career, when I was primarily focussed on what I was teaching and how well (or otherwise) the children were grasping it. For instance, last month I took part in a 'Review and Development' discussion about the problems we're having at wet breaktimes. Wet breaks are one of the things most, if not all, teachers dread. It's not only the wet breaks themselves, but also the decision to call one in the first place, and the ramifications for the rest of the day that worry us. Behaviour after a wet break or lunchtime is notoriously more difficult to manage; children need time and space to let off steam, and for some drawing or reading just doesn't cut it.

So, who takes the decision to declare a 'Wet Break'? Should it be a senior member of staff, or the teachers on break duty that day? If the former, what about if that person is not in school? How heavy does the rain have to be to confine the troops to barracks? Do we have sufficient resources in each classroom to keep the pupils occupied indoors? What are appropriate and inappropriate activities for wet breaks? Should we, at lunchtime, just head for the sanctuary of the staff room and leave all supervisory duties to the dinner ladies (and our solitary dinner man)? What about a quiet room for those struggling with the noise and hi-jinks in their own rooms?

The group of teachers I was with had a lively discussion about all these matters. We came up with a set of guidelines which will be added to the Staff Handbook. Amongst our conclusions were a budget of £10 for each class to buy wet play games, a rota for teachers to help the beleaguered dinner ladies and a request to stick to a decision on a wet play and not keep chopping and changing!

Chapter 7

"We don't want to see you go,
but we think you should!"

Monday, 5th October 1992

This is now, unbelievably, already my 7th year of teaching. But I know this term will be my last term at Lyndhurst. I will be moving to a new school after Christmas. I've loved working here but realise, for several reasons, I can't stay here forever. From fairly early on in my time here, inspired not only by our brilliant Deputy Head John, but also by other senior colleagues, I've felt I could be a Deputy and would quite like to test myself and see if I could do it. Headship- not sure, but a Deputy, yes. Of course this would mean a lot more responsibility, but it would also mean more money. Nobody comes in to teaching to be well off (they'll soon be disappointed if they do!), but teaching salaries are respectable in my eyes and moving up the ladder will be handy if we decide to have children, which might be a consideration in the not-too-distant future.

So, for the last couple of years, I've been dipping my toe in the water and applying for quite a few Deputy or Assistant Head jobs. It's been an interesting, if at times frustrating process. You come to realise that it's as much about the qualities and talents of your fellow candidates as it is about your own. If they have more experience in an area the recruiting school is after, then they're likely to get the nod ahead of you. The fact I've only ever worked in one school has counted against me, as all my answers are based on how things are done at Lyndhurst (memories of my teaching practice schools are already fading fast.) So, whilst I've made it as far as a few interviews, as yet I haven't been successful in getting a job with 'head' in the title.

The other issue is the type of school I'm in. Middle schools, be they the 9-13 or 8-12 variety, are still popular in some authorities (my beloved Dorset being one), but Hertfordshire, the authority I'm working for, has only ever dabbled in them. There's a handful of them in towns around the edge of the county. The arrival of the National Curriculum, the establishment of the Key Stages, and the increase in school accountability have proved problematic for them because they don't really fit into this new system. We can argue at the end of KS2 that all the damage was done at the feeder First School if standards are not up to scratch, and similarly the Upper School can blame us for poor standards if results are below par at KS3. I sense the powers that be are not comfortable with this state of affairs.

Now, I think Middle Schools are great. Yes, they mean children will have two moves in their school lives instead of one, but they mean children are exposed to specialist teaching at an earlier stage (when I was working in what is now called Year 6, my class would have benefited very little from me teaching them the likes of Music, Art or Design Technology.) Also, they're small enough to offer a good standard (I like to think!) of pastoral care at a crucial stage of the pupils' development. This is not to say that colleagues in all through Secondary (11-18) schools can't do this, but some of them are so vast, some children must surely 'fall through the cracks.'

However, the reality is that Middle Schools are likely to be phased out in the future, especially in authorities where they're not county wide, so I feel a decision needs to be made as to whether I see my long-term future in Primary (4-11) or Secondary (11-18) schools. I'm worried about the pressures of maintaining discipline and preparing children for exams in Secondary schools, so I'm leaning towards Primary.

To this end, I applied for the Deputy Headship at a Junior (7-11) school in Radlett last term. 'Standalone' Junior schools are relatively rare but there are a few about, and they offer me the added advantage of not having to deal with very young children, who to me are every bit as scary as unruly teenagers! Radlett is a small town only a couple of miles north of Borehamwood. It's the next stop on the 'Bedpan'

(Bedford to St Pancras) railway line. They offered the job to an internal candidate, but I must've made some sort of favourable impression, because the Head made me an interesting offer.

Would I be interested in joining his team as 'Senior Teacher'? This would be a 'sideways move', still on a 'B' allowance, but part of the Senior Leadership Team, effectively third in command in the school, with special responsibility for developing Assessment, an area that does interest me. This was a new post the school were talking about creating for me here, so I felt it needed serious consideration.

I promised him a decision in a week. It wasn't an easy choice, and it involved some agonising discussions with family, friends and colleagues, but in the end, I said yes with an eye on the hopefully long-term benefits it will bring my future job prospects. More experience in a different setting and a greater depth to my answers in future Deputy Headship interviews. So, I accepted the job with effect from January next year. But even now, although looking forward to the challenge, I'm worried about missing a school and colleagues I've really come to value.

I think back over the last six years to all the lessons I've learnt from my colleagues, people who in some cases I know I'll be thinking "what would X do?" for the rest of my career. The great Year 2 team spirit with Carole and Nikki in those early years. The sheer professionalism and skill of Mark and Yvonne. The resilience under fire of Shirley and John. The 'esprit de corps' fostered in our daily morning briefings, and the parting words of "be careful out there", like the sergeant at the end of his pep talks in *Hill Street Blues*.

I think back too to all the fun we've had. The light-hearted moments that keep you going when you're having a tough week. Like the time when the staff ribbed me mercilessly that I was going to be poisoned by a child with a very challenging background from our EBD unit who had chosen me to cook a meal for one lunchtime as part of his social skills education. Or the boy in my first ever class who got his words a bit muddled one morning and politely asked, "Excuse me Mr Toilet, may I go to the hall?" Or the morning after a staff social event, when a large number of us phoned up the school answerphone to say we were unwell, and sneaked into school early, parking out of sight, hiding ourselves away in the room next door to hear our long-suffering Deputy Head John playing the messages, but then our sniggering giving us away in the end. Or Mel, our ageing mild-mannered music teacher, failing to appear at the piano on cue during a school panto, and requiring a highly embarrassed staff choir to sing acapella to a packed hall of parents laughing uncontrollably. And, the time when he was unwise enough to sleep in his car overnight at a chess tournament, and end up being questioned by police about a murder that had taken place locally that night.

Tonight, chatting after the staff meeting, my Headteacher Shirley, picking up on my doubts, says, "We don't want to see you go, but we think you should." Her way of saying I need to move to advance my career. Anyway, there's no going back now- the contract is signed and come the New Year, I'll be plying my trade in School No 2.

Chapter 8

"Bluff your way in Teaching."

Wednesday, 13th October 1993

Today I'm spending half of the day out of school on a training course. So, having wolfed down my lunch, I jump in the car and drive for half an hour or so to the Wheathampstead Education Centre, where most of the training for Hertfordshire teachers currently takes place. It's an old secondary school campus and provides not only a daily programme of training courses, but is also home to a large collection of resources, which we can borrow and keep at our schools for a while if we so choose.

This afternoon's course is about planning our Geography curriculum. Already, I'm appreciating the fact that I'm now teaching in a school that covers just one Key Stage (in our case, KS2.) This means that as long as we follow the guidelines/ constraints (depending on your viewpoint) of the National Curriculum, we are free to choose the content and skills that we teach in school. There is no need to barter with colleagues from other local schools about what we're doing, because they have their own Key Stages and their own guidelines/ constraints.

I should also explain that in a Junior School like ours, as was the case in my previous school too, each curriculum area is the responsibility of a teacher. This person has an overview of what is taught across the school in that subject and tries to ensure that it is planned logically and that the skills taught progress in terms of difficulty as the children move up the school. The 'Curriculum Co-ordinator', as they are known, is also expected to keep abreast of any developments in the subject, and to advise colleagues about how to approach the teaching of the subject.

In a small school like ours, there are only six class teachers, and there are twelve subjects to be covered, so most teachers have at least two areas of responsibility; some may have three, as the Maths and English co-ordinators have enough on their plates with just the one subject and it is not usually expected for them to take on another one. Anyway, one of my subjects is Geography, which is why I'm heading off to this course.

I'm quite happy with being the Geography co-ordinator, as I've always been into maps and stuff. I even possess two 'O' Levels in the subject. I got a solid pass when I was 16 but then messed up my 'A' Level two years later and got an 'O' grade- not good enough to scrape a pass, but not bad enough for it to be the dreaded 'U' (was that ungraded or unclassified?) At the time, the thought that my geographical knowledge had not moved on one iota in two years had been hard to take, but I think I'm over it now. I probably won't mention it to my fellow Geography Co-ordinators this afternoon though!

En route to the course, I reflect on my first ten months or so at Fair Field. After this length of time, I'm gradually beginning to feel that I made the right decision to move, although those early months back at the start of the year were tough.

In January, I was faced with teaching children who, in some cases, were five years younger than the children I had been teaching just before the Christmas break. This was a massive culture shock in terms of what the children could achieve in a lesson, and I've had to revise my expectations accordingly. Progress in learning seemed desperately slow at first, but some of my class were two years younger than I'd ever taught before, so of course it was going to be very different. I'm now more practised in matters like tying shoelaces, finding lost items and in one memorable case, extricating a pupil from a toilet cubicle after she'd somehow managed to lock herself in!

That first class (and indeed this next one too) also provided me with two extra new challenges. Firstly, they are what's called a 'vertically grouped' class. We have around 45 children in each year group- not enough for two whole classes but too many for just one.

That means that around 15 of the 45 are taught with 15 of a year group either a year older or a year younger than them. So, I have a class that is half Y3 and half Y4. In some cases, the children have an almost two-year age gap, and this provides challenges, especially in subjects like maths, when it comes to ensuring that the difficulty of the learning is pitched correctly.

Secondly, because I'm now teaching in a Junior School, there's no palming off my children to other teachers when it comes to my less confident subjects. Those days are over; I'm doing the lot. Art, Technology, Music, everything. This is slightly worrying, and a source of amusement to my friends and family, who are aware of my lack of interest in, and aptitude for, these parts of the curriculum. There's a popular series of books around at the moment called the *'Bluff your way in.....'* series. I was presented with a copy of the *'Teaching'* volume of the series by a colleague at my previous school, and when it comes to these lessons, I feel there's been a fair bit of 'bluffing' going on. My tactics basically consist of blagging ideas from colleagues, making a joke of my abilities with the class, planning carefully and keeping my fingers firmly crossed.

So far it seems to be working, and this is partly due to my lovely new colleagues, who, I soon find out, are unsurprisingly in a similar situation. My two fellow Y3/4 teachers, Sue and Marilyn are, fortunately, gifted in music and art respectively, so I can always tap them up for ideas and hopefully reciprocate on occasions when it comes to areas I know a bit more about. This afternoon's course provides not only some good ideas on planning the KS2 Geography curriculum, but also a few nuggets that might help with individual lessons, so I dutifully make a note of them in the hope they will be swappable for some insights into musical scales or artistic tones.

Chapter 9

Secondary Transfer and a Withdrawn Bus Pass.

Monday, October 10th 1994

Given my relatively senior status in my new school, I have been invited along to a number of Governors' meetings during the last couple of years. I've mainly been observing, but occasionally I've been able to contribute an observation or an idea. This has been yet another level of 'eye-opening' for me. Governors discuss important stuff to do with schools which as an ordinary classroom teacher, you don't really think about, most of the time anyway. It's all very useful to me in terms of seeing the 'bigger picture' and getting an insight into some of the behind-the-scenes discussions and decisions that need to be taken that keep a school running. A lot of these come down to money. Can we afford a new part time teacher to help support some of our children's learning? Have we got enough lunchtime supervisory staff? Can we put together a realistic bid for a new classroom as the school numbers are expanding, or will we have to make do with our existing accommodation? I'm working with one of the Governors, Ken, to see if it is possible to secure some grants for an artificial cricket strip to be installed on the field.

The Governors are an impressive group of people. Most of them are not from an educational background, but they grasp the challenges of running a school with amazing intelligence, and provide, it seems to me, a useful balance of challenge and support to my great new boss, Doug. Tonight is one of the most important nights of the year for the Governors. It's their AGM, and parents are allowed to attend. This meeting currently must happen by law. In order to boost attendance figures, and ensure the meeting is useful rather than just a meeting for a meetings sake, two local secondary headteachers have been invited to speak on the thorny subject of Secondary Transfer.

The situation as regards this aspect of school life could not be more different to the situation I had been used to at Lyndhurst. In Borehamwood, the vast majority of our Y8 leavers toddled off to one of the two Upper Schools in the town, and that was that. In fact, most went to the school that was on our side of town because it was the most convenient. Other than saying goodbye in July, the whole process barely impacted on me and, as far as I could tell, was pretty straightforward for the parents and the school admin staff too.

In Radlett, though, it's a whole different ball game. Radlett is either a small town or a large village, depending on your viewpoint. Either way, because of its relatively small size, it doesn't have a secondary school. It being on the edge of London and close to other large population centres, however, there are lots of possible secondary school options nearby. I was amazed to find out that Fair Field regularly sends its leavers to around fifteen different schools. There are state schools in nearby Watford and St Albans to consider. Some of the schools in Watford are 'selective' and require prospective pupils to sit an entrance exam. There are also a number of private school options locally- I've already taken sports teams to Haberdashers and Aldenham schools, for example.

The early part of Year 6 involves our pupils and their parents in lots of visits to possible schools, and ultimately a difficult decision and important forms to fill out. The most important piece of advice given by our Headteacher visitors is to make sure that the forms are returned on time; if they aren't your chances of securing a place at the school of your choice will be much reduced. They also suggest visiting possible schools during the day, as this will give a better feel for what a school is really like, rather than just attending a set piece Open Evening type event. An obvious point, I suppose, but not one I'd really appreciated.

Parents are told that if the school is a Grant Maintained school (this means one that has opted out of LEA control and is funded directly by a grant from central government), then they will have their own forms and criteria for admission. Their forms need returning directly to them, whereas the LEA form needs returning to the Fair Field school office, where our secretary will pass them onto the admissions team at County Hall in Hertford.

It is explained that all admission criteria at all schools should be objective. How well have you done in our entrance exam? Do you have a sibling already here? Do you already attend one of our traditional feeder schools? How far is your home address from our school? Do we have facilities that will help meet a particular need of yours (such as a hearing-impaired unit, for example)?

The distance issue reminds me of a strange episode from my youth which my Mum and Dad still remind me of from time to time. When I started secondary school in September 1975, I was given a bus pass to cover my fares because my house was more than three miles from my school. This was measured, I think, door to door by the most direct road route. Towards the end of that term, we received a letter from the LEA to say that the distance had been re-measured, and from January my bus pass was being withdrawn. I think Dad appealed to the council and argued, not unreasonably, that neither the school nor the house had moved and it seemed an unfair judgement. However, the council refused to budge and as we knew it was pretty borderline, we didn't make any further fuss and I just paid the fare (which from memory rose from 3p to 25p each way during the seven years that I took the journey.)

Back in the Governors meeting for parents, our audience is told that each school will have an Appeals Committee, to which you can turn if you're not offered a place at your preferred school. Their main job is to decide how many extra places the school could reasonably offer without the education of those already admitted suffering. A tricky balancing act if ever there was one.

Despite the anxiety you can see written on the parents' faces, they are clearly appreciative of the advice, the time of the Headteachers and the efforts of the Governors to facilitate the meeting, so it's been a successful evening for the school and one that has taught me a lot about another aspect of the education world.

Chapter 10

Tough on your average ten- or eleven-year-old.

Wednesday, October 4th 1995

This morning, I'm experiencing a curious mixture of excitement and fear. Excitement as I have a chance to showcase some of the good work myself and my colleagues have been doing, but fear that I might be exposed as not quite the expert I thought I was. We're welcoming some teachers from other schools to Fair Field for what's known as an 'Agreement Trialling' session.

This is an activity that falls very much within my area of responsibility- assessment. Over the last three years, I like to think I've moved the school on in this area and have certainly received a lot of encouragement and praise from Doug, my Headteacher. Doug is a visionary. He leaves most of the day-to-day minutiae of the running of the school to his excellent Deputy, Carol, while he pushes the school forward towards the twenty first century, an aim he is assisted in by my colleague Paul, a whizzkid when it comes to computers and fearless experimenter with how new technologies can be used in the classroom. Doug will be present this morning as we look at examples of children's written work and try and agree on their levels. It's all part of efforts by the LEA, and ultimately the government, to try and ensure that standards are consistently applied across schools.

The area of assessment has seen massive changes over recent years. Again, this all stems from the Education Act of 1988. The new National Curriculum had to be seen to be a good thing, so in the so called 'core' subjects of English, Maths and Science, even down at lowly Key Stage 2, tests (they're exams really, sat under strict rules) have been set for the children at the end of the key stage (at Year 6, when children are 10 or 11 years old.) This has allowed the government

2 5

(and the LEA) to compare schools, and, in some ways, pit them against each other. I've felt this on a personal level, because after just five terms teaching the Y3/4 class, internal changes meant I was moved to teach a Y6 class, so last summer my class did their SATs, as they're becoming known. SATs stands for Standard Assessment Tasks.

SATs take place across the whole of England and Wales during a pre-planned week in May. There are writing, reading and spelling tests in English. There are two written maths papers, plus a mental arithmetic test that we play to the children on a tape recorder. There are two science papers as well. So, a total of eight exams in five days. That's tough on your average ten- or eleven-year-old. My own last year at primary school (now twenty years ago!) did involve me doing the Eleven Plus, but that was it, and I certainly didn't have my teacher banging on about it all academic year, as I fear I was guilty of last year!

The government have also introduced a system of levels. At Key Stage 2, the expected level of attainment is Level 4. And that's crucial when it comes to the reporting of our results to the wider world; the % of our children who achieve Level 4 or above is what is published. So, a school might have 75% in English, 78% in Maths and 72% in Science, for example. This is where the element of competition comes in- if other local schools perform significantly better, that might be a problem for you. Tricky questions could well be asked of the staff by parents, Governors and LEA advisers, with the former possibly voting with their feet and looking at alternative schools for their offspring.

This has ratcheted up the pressure on the children and the staff. Overall, I was pleased with the scores my children achieved last term, but inevitably there were a few who I felt didn't quite do justice to themselves in some of the papers. One poor girl missed out on getting her Level 4 reading by just one mark. When the papers are returned to the school, we have the chance to look again at borderline cases, and appeal if we think it's appropriate. I checked her scripts and noticed that she had not been given a mark for one particular question because she had included a telephone number at the bottom of an address when asked to write what she would put on an envelope when writing to a particular person mentioned in a non-fiction text. My argument was the envelope would still have been delivered safely even though the telephone number was superfluous. The appeal failed, so that particular young lady will now go through life with it on her records that she did not make the required standard in reading at the end of her primary education!

However, in order to provide balance in the case of such potential injustices, us teachers also provide a Teacher Assessment Level for each of the core subjects as well. Hence, today's meeting, which will be run by a member of the Herts Advisory staff. A colleague from Fair Field and I will be bringing along samples of what we think are Levels 3, 4 and 5 writing, as will a number of teachers from other schools. We will then check these against the writing attainment targets, and either agree with the suggested level, or adjust them up or down as appropriate. The idea is that by looking at a range of work from different schools, we will become more skilled at assessing the level of our own children's work.

Another potential issue or concern is that the tests will cause a 'narrowing' of the primary curriculum. Unfortunately, I think there's probably a grain of truth in this. If I'm honest, there have been a few occasions in recent times when a Foundation (non-core) Subject has slipped off the conveyor belt and not happened because I've been spending more time with the class making sure that they've grasped a concept in Maths, English or Science that might come up in the SATs. People not doing our job are saying it's important to keep a broad and balanced curriculum and that under no circumstances must we 'teach to the test.' But people not doing our job are not being judged on that % score, so it's easy for them to say that.

I reflect on all these changes as I speed down the M1 a little earlier than usual, not only because I'm anxious to get into school and get all set up early for the Agreement Trialling, but because for the first time in weeks I do not have my baby daughter Rosie in the car for company. Rosie arrived with an impeccable sense of timing on the Monday of last February's half term. This meant I had the whole of that week (and two days of the next one that Doug generously gave to me on compassionate grounds) to get my head round being a Dad and provide support to my wife, Sarah.

During the summer, we found an excellent child minder who is also a parent at the school just round the corner from where I work, so Rosie has been my early morning companion since the start of term. Today, though, is Yom Kippur and Michele is otherwise engaged so Rosie is elsewhere.

The Agreement Trialling, when it happens, passes off satisfactorily enough from my point of view. One of my pieces of work gets downgraded, but generally my judgements are felt to be sound, and I hold my own in the discussions competently enough I feel and learn a lot from the other teachers. My knowledge of all those writing attainment targets is certainly growing. Doug and the adviser seem happy enough with the outcome, and I head back to class for afternoon lessons content and relieved.

Chapter 11

Making a Statement.

Tuesday, 15th October 1996

One of the areas of teaching that I know I need to improve on is my support for, and understanding of, children with Special Educational Needs. Although I consider myself to be an empathetic person, I do sometimes struggle to grasp the reasons why pupils struggle with classroom tasks. For example, I can look at the working behind a child's wrong answer to a maths problem for quite a while and still be none the wiser as to their misconception. In English, I get frustrated when children can't write in sentences- but teaching what a sentence is to young children involves quite a lot of dry grammar stuff that I can't remember learning. I realise that my knowledge of what constitutes a sentence comes from reading a lot as a child, and yet again I realise I have a lot to thank Dad for when he dutifully tore out the sports pages of *The Daily Telegraph* each morning before heading off to work.

Today, I have a lunchtime meeting with someone who is far more skilled in all this than me. I am meeting our brilliant SENCO, Chris. I should explain that since another Education Act (this one a few years ago in 1993), by law every school must have a SENCO (Special Educational Needs Co-ordinator.) This person is responsible for managing everything to do with SEN in the school on a day-to-day basis. It's a daunting prospect and takes a special kind of person to do it well. Despite my leadership aspirations, I am already very clear after a decade in the profession that I could never join the ranks of this band of saints.

Amongst other things, the SENCO needs to make sure our SEN policy is followed, liaise with parents and teachers to support SEN pupils, keep detailed and up to date records of their progress, and co-ordinate the writing of Statements of Special Educational Needs.

This last item is the reason for our meeting today. A Statement of Special Educational Needs is a very important document. If your child has one (and, as I understand it, they're not at all easy to get and involve a lot of work by parents, SEN and advisory staff), it has a legal status. We have just three of our pupils in receipt of one at the moment in a school with around two hundred on roll.

The Statement will include detailed information on the child's needs, the education setting they should attend and how they will be supported there. Twenty years or so ago, many of these children would have been in Special Schools, but there has been a trend towards integrating more children into 'mainstream schools', and in general this is seen as a good thing in the education world, as it promotes a more inclusive and cohesive society. Certainly, I have seen the benefits for a number of SEN children from integrating with others in this way, but it comes with the caveat that the schools need to be properly resourced so that they can provide appropriate support.

Our meeting today is because a statement review, which must happen annually, is coming up for a child in my class. We talk at length about how K is doing, and if there are any extra hours of Gerry's (our Welfare Assistant) time, that we might be able to assign to her. Chris reinforces with me some important teaching tips for K, particularly around her processing of instructions. I make some notes and promise to get it all written up over half term ready for the review meeting during the first week back.

It's been an interesting month. The other day Doug popped into my room one afternoon and said that we had received notification that OFSTED will be visiting the school next April, with a visit starting on the 14th. So, we have six months to get our house in order and make sure that everything at Fair Field is all singing, all dancing. I wasn't overly pleased with the date because it happens to be the 'due date' when Sarah is expecting our second child. I don't think I'll be getting two days compassionate leave this time!

OFSTED inspections have been going a few years now and I guess it was just a matter of time before our school was chosen. There have been some criticisms of the system in the educational press, but Doug is bullish about the challenge and is determined that we will use the visit to show the school at its best. For my part, I am reasonably used to being observed by senior colleagues and advisory staff, but completely detached inspectors is a new one on me.

In my first year of teaching, I was chosen completely at random to be visited by an HMI (Her Majesty's Inspector) as part of a survey called *The New Teacher in School*. I remember having to fill out a detailed questionnaire before his arrival, and on the day, he observed absolutely everything I did, including a PE lesson on the field in a fierce rainstorm. He graded my teaching, but I never found out which grade I fell into, as everything was anonymised in the final report. So, this will be a whole new level of accountability and public scrutiny for us to face.

Chapter 12

Mentoring the Next Generation.

Tuesday, 7th October 1997

It's another half day out of the classroom for me today. This time, after lunch, I make the short drive to Wall Hall College. This is a building just outside Radlett with an interesting history. It has associations with both world wars, having been used as a hospital for wounded soldiers in the First, and as a training centre for the Special Operations Executive in the Second. Nowadays, however, it has a function that, I would argue, is almost as important as nursing wounded heroes or teaching special agents the finer points of propaganda techniques. It is a teacher training college, and I'm invited here this afternoon as I will soon be working with a student teacher, Tammy, back in my classroom at Fair Field.

There are now two main routes into teaching. The first route, generally favoured by those like me in the primary sector, is to obtain a Bachelor of Education (BEd) degree. The second is to obtain a specialised degree in, say Geography, and then do a Postgraduate Certificate in Education (PGCE); this is the more common route for Secondary teachers. There are still quite a few teachers in the system with an old-style Certificate of Education (CertEd), but this qualification was phased out in the ten years or so before I started my training in 1982, as there was a drive to make teaching a 'graduate only' profession. My own view is that having a degree rather than a certificate makes very little difference to your ability to do the job effectively, and many of the CertEd teachers I've come across during my career have been very good indeed.

Anyhow, Tammy is doing the BEd course at Wall Hall, and for her sins has been placed with me for the next couple of months. I've taken it as a compliment that Doug and Carol have asked me to take on this role, as presumably they feel that I will be at least a passable role-model for her. Schools are under no formal obligation to take student teachers, but all training courses require a degree of actual practice in the classroom, so if schools refused to do so the whole system would break down pretty quickly. We're fairly close to the college, so the school has a recent history of taking a steady stream of students. It's generally agreed that, although it's a fair bit of work for the 'host' school, we do benefit as well from the input of youthful enthusiasm and up to date knowledge that the students usually bring to a school.

Doug is keen for us to keep moving forward as a school, and working with students is one way we can all improve our own skills as well as nurturing the next generation of teachers. Last term's long awaited OFSTED inspection was generally positive- we were described as an "improving, well led school where pupils and adults work hard." Inevitably, though, there were areas in which the report thought we could do better, and these now form part of the School Development Plan and are a constant back drop to our daily tasks.

One bizarre occurrence during the inspection was that part of the way through it, the inspectors had to relocate their hotel base, and the new accommodation was at Luton Airport, not far from where I live. I offered to meet them there one morning so that they could follow me into work, as I've become a bit of an expert at using the back roads to avoid the M1 if the tailbacks become too onerous. Arriving a little earlier than scheduled with Rosie in tow, we briefly sat with them at their breakfast table. Rosie was her usual lively and inquisitive self and upset a glass of orange juice, which almost found its way onto the smart suit trousers of one of our distinguished visitors. That would not have helped the report much I'm sure!

Meanwhile, back at Wall Hall College, the afternoon is a mix of administrative information about what teaching the student should ideally be doing when, and practical guidance on how to be an effective mentor. I will need to be overseeing her lesson plans, observing her teaching the lessons and ultimately writing a report for the college on how well she's done at the end of the placement. The college will also be sending in a tutor to watch Tammy teach. And she'll of course get the chance to observe me teach as well.

As I'm taking all this in, and making some notes on the dos and don'ts, my mind drifts back to my own days as a student teacher. During my four-year course, I had five placements ranging in duration from a fortnight to a whole term. Three in middle schools, one in a junior school and one in a secondary school. I do remember, about half an hour into my first ever day in school as a student, sitting on a windowsill watching in wonder the class teacher having the almost silent pupils eating out of her hand while she explained the next task of the day. I shuffled slightly uncomfortably and managed to send a pot of pencils crashing across the classroom and completely shattered the peace. I could feel my face reddening as the pupils turned to face me. Not the greatest start, certainly. But I recovered to enjoy a happy pre-Christmas fortnight with that class, and I even managed to hitch a free ride back to London with them on a coach at the start of the holidays, as they were coming up to the BBC to film an episode of *Finders Keepers* with Richard Stilgoe. I secured my passage by offering my services as an extra supervising adult on the journey, but in the event, I spent most of the time asleep as I'd taken a healthy dose of travel sickness tablets.

The following summer, in my only foray into the world of secondary schools, I spent a tricky fortnight teaching mainly history and geography. As a nineteen-year-old at the time, some of my classes featured pupils only a few years my junior. Particularly embarrassing was a moment when I was writing on the board with my back turned to the class and could hear a few girls in the front row giving my backside marks out of ten. Some of the marks were embarrassing in themselves, but I also found myself at a loss as to how to deal with this and merely carried spouting on about Britain during The Blitz, or whatever it was.

I also recall that corporal punishment was (just) still legal while I was a student teacher. In fact, it became illegal during the year I qualified, 1986. During the years immediately before this date, it was generally accepted to belong to a different time and be on the way out and was almost certainly used more sparingly than in previous eras. But in one of my teaching practice schools, it was still used, and I recall the buzz going round the school when word got out that so and so had had the slipper/ cane or was just about to.

I'm looking forward to the next couple of months. Tammy strikes me as a pretty capable student, and I think it's unlikely that there'll be many issues with getting her to pass this part of her course. In some ways, it might give me a bit of time to breathe and pace myself through the rest of this term. And I undoubtedly do need to pace myself. We've now welcomed another new addition to our family. Lottie arrived a month earlier than planned so as it turned out I was off work for the Easter fortnight not long after she was born. But with Sarah now already back at work, it's tough at times having the energy and logistical skills to cope. One day a couple of weeks ago, I was forced to bring Lottie (at six months old) into the classroom for the day as our child minder was ill and we had nowhere else for her to be. Cue a maths lesson investigating the frequency of her nappy usage and instructional writing on how to change a nappy. She won't remember that day of course, but I certainly won't forget it in a hurry, and I like to think it might stick in the mind of at least some of the pupils for a while as well.

Chapter 13

The death of ERIC?

Friday, October 9th 1998

This morning my class, UJH (it stands for Upper Juniors- that's them and Hall- that's me) are giving a poetry recital to the rest of the school and their parents. It's not just us- other classes will be performing as well. This is part of a big push that, along with other schools, we are having this year in English. Except it's not called English anymore. It's been re-christened Literacy. And since the beginning of term, schools have been delivering something each day which is being called the 'Literacy Hour.' This is an initiative that schools are being told is not statutory, but if you don't do it, you must be able to show inspectors, advisers and the like that your alternative is at least as effective. Not surprisingly, most schools are adopting the 'Literacy Hour.'

The new Labour Government elected last year are hot on standards in schools; less than a year before his landslide victory, Mr Blair had stated that his three main priorities if elected would be "education, education and education." We have a new Education Secretary (David Blunkett), who is already the sixth holder of that office since I joined the profession a dozen years ago. Teachers can easily become cynical about the Secretary of State and their capacity to know what they're talking about when it comes to education. I remember with a smile my dear ex-colleague Cynthia on the day John MacGregor was made Education Secretary in 1989. "Oh my God!", she exclaimed, "they've sent us another one from Ag and Fish- what does he know about teaching?!"

One of our INSET (training) days at the start of term last month was completely given over to training about the new Literacy Hour, and Sally, our LEA adviser, came to deliver it to us. Apparently, latest research indicates that primary age children (especially boys) will benefit from a more structured approach to the teaching of reading, writing, speaking and listening skills. The government are, in particular, concerned about how much time is spent on free reading with little or no intervention from the teacher.

Amongst most of my colleagues, this is a controversial view. The merits of a short (say 15-20 minutes) daily session where everyone in the class just sits reading quietly are twofold. First, it can provide a valuable way of settling a class after a lunchtime of boisterous play. Secondly, it can help foster a love of reading for its own sake. There have certainly been periods of time where class teachers have even been encouraged to not listen to readers during this time, but read to themselves in full view of the class, the theory being that this shows to the children the value of reading, even to adults. However, we need to concede that we are working in an area of the country where the majority of children are keen readers anyway and probably have a healthy supply of books in the home; maybe such sessions would be of less value in inner city or more deprived areas where the basics of reading are not yet embedded.

Either way, it seems the days of ERIC ("Everybody reading in class") are numbered. I remember that some years ago we had some fun coming up with other possible names for these sessions. GRAHAM ("General reading amidst hardly a murmur") was a favourite, but RICHARD ("Reading in class having a right doss") suggests that perhaps there is a grain of truth in the concerns of the powers that be.

So, the Literacy Hour. This really is a prescriptive method of teaching. It's a far cry from what Mr Williams, my own Year 6 teacher all those years ago, would have considered an appropriate English lesson. Each Literacy hour is to be divided into four distinct sections.

For the first 15 minutes, we will be engaged in 'Shared reading or writing.' We will be reading from a text (possibly one of the newly purchased 'Big Books', which are large enough for the children to see even from the back of the carpet), and then using that stimulus to create whole class poems, stories or reports. The training said that this initial text should be too hard for most pupils, so it is stretching them and expanding their vocabulary.

Next, we will move onto 15 minutes of 'Word or Sentence' work; this is essentially the grammar and punctuation bit. Thirdly, there will be 20 minutes of guided reading or writing that will be done in ability groups. Each member of the group should have a copy of a book or text, in this case 95% understandable to the pupils. Finally, there is a 10-minute plenary in which we review what we've done and assess what we've achieved. So, there you go: 15+15+20+10=60- one hour of quality Literacy teaching to raise standards.

This morning's poetry recital is an early chance to showcase what we've been doing in the Literacy Hour. We've created a whole class poem based on some we've been reading, redrafted it together and then learnt it; some verses are being performed by the whole class and some by small groups. I am pleased with the outcome and most of the children seem to quite enjoy the experience. The jury is out on The Literacy Hour for now though. It might help to raise standards in some areas of the country, but at what cost to the collective blood pressures of the teaching fraternity? Already some of us are struggling with the prescriptive nature of the changing from one activity to another in such a strict manner and more than once the plenary has in practice been "Oh shit, it's time for assembly, let's go!" This of course has been the thought process rather than the actual words uttered to the class!

Chapter 14

That 'Brian Hanrahan moment'.

Tuesday, October 19th 1999

It's a school trip day today. I always have mixed feelings about these. On the one hand, it's a welcome change of routine. A chance to take the pupils to a different setting, get out of the classroom, and hopefully let them see their learning come alive. On the other hand, it's a real responsibility. In my experience, children are generally easier to control when within the confines of four walls than when allowed to roam freely outside them. The possibilities of less-than-ideal behaviour (in full view of the Great British public), serious injury and even losing one of your class seem to be magnified once you leave the school premises.

Today's destination is a potentially fascinating one. As part of Year 6's RE work on Hinduism, we are visiting the mandir (temple) in Neasden, North London. I've visited nearby Wembley Stadium several times for football matches, but this architectural wonder has so far passed me by. The pictures look breathtaking, and I'm even more intrigued by the fact that all the stonework was hand carved in India before being sent to London for assembling over here.

The children I will be accompanying today are from Class 6H in my new school that I joined last month. After several years of trying, last February I finally secured that elusive Deputy Headship, and am now the proud holder of that job title at Bishop Wood Church of England Junior School in Tring, tucked away in the northwestern corner of Hertfordshire.

I had applied for the job when living temporarily with friends whilst coming to terms with an unsettling change in my domestic circumstances, and at the time didn't feel I'd given the application as much attention as it perhaps deserved. Nevertheless, I'd done enough on paper to secure a place on the shortlist, and when the interview day came, I found myself warming to the task and revelling in the chance it gave me to focus on something other than my home issues. I felt I did OK in both interviews, and particularly enjoyed meeting the School Council pupils. At the end of the day, I accepted the offer of the job with a mixture of relief, delight and surprise. My new boss Brian told me much later that it had been close between me and one of the other candidates, but he had chosen me because I was the one that was least like him- an interesting take on successful leadership teams that I hadn't thought of before.

So, in the summer, I had to say a sad goodbye to another team of teachers that I'd come to really enjoy being with. The decision seven years ago to swap Lyndhurst for Fair Field had been the right one- not only because it had ultimately got me the Deputy Headship, but because it had taught me a whole new load of stuff about teaching, and given me many more great memories. The Governors and Staff cricket matches, the fantastic school productions (even if Doug had only just got over the cost of the curtain cleaning after the over-enthusiastic use of the splurge guns in *Bugsy Malone*), the school residential trips to Cuffley Camp and the Isle of Wight, the end of year parties in the school swimming pool when we drank champagne off the swimming floats and fantasised about six weeks without a learning objective or a break duty in sight. The time when two of my fun-loving colleagues mocked up a very convincing letter purporting to come from the Civil Aviation Authority and sent it to Doug giving him a very firm rap on the knuckles about the school's recent charity balloon release. All great fun and things I will remember forever.

However, all good things must come to an end as the saying goes, and as we head down the A41 towards the temple, it is my new class and the challenges of my new school that I am focussing on. When we arrive, the mandir does not disappoint. The beautifully intricate and startingly white structure is really quite stunning. Inside, we learn more about how it was built, how it is used on a day-to-day basis by the local Hindu community, and get to see some of the sacred images that Hindus use in their daily acts of worship. Most importantly from an RE point of view, we actually get to witness some of these take place during our visit, and I catch some of my class in moments of genuine 'awe and wonder' as they sit fascinated watching what's going on. Overall, I'm pleased with their behaviour, and they don't make too much fuss when told they will have to remove their shoes whilst inside the building.

Like all children though, 6H only really have two things on their minds when on a school trip. When is lunch, and when can we go to the shop? We tackle the second of these first, and they enjoy spending their few pounds that they've been allowed to bring along in the well stocked souvenir shop. Then, we hop back onto the coach and head over to the nearby Welsh Harp reservoir, where they can stretch their legs and eat their lunch. The skies are leaden and it's none too warm, but at least the rain holds off, and before long we're counting the children back onto the coach for the return journey back to Tring. I always experience a huge sense of relief when the coach sets off on the way back at the end of a school trip. I've come to think of it as my 'Brian Hanrahan moment' after the famous quote from the BBC reporter when describing fighter planes on a raid during the Falklands War, "I counted them all out and I counted them all back." I will sleep well tonight.

Chapter 15

South East London or North West Kent?

Thursday, 19th October 2000

Today Brian and I are meeting our County Adviser, Mo, for a target setting meeting. This takes place every year around this time and involves setting targets for the Year 6 children who will be taking their SATs next May.

I like Mo. She is very driven and clearly has a genuine passion for education and helping schools do their best for the pupils in their care. She is the third or so adviser that I've got to know reasonably well and like the others, the difficulty I have with her is that she's just a bit too bright for me. Almost every time I meet her, she asks me at least one question that I have no idea how to answer, sometimes because it's about something I haven't even considered before.

Advisers are an interesting bunch. In many respects, I admire them, as they're setting themselves up as experts, and some teachers can be cynically dismissive of their ideas as not being 'doable' in the real world of day-to-day classroom activity. Largely for this reason, like becoming a SENCO, I've already completely dismissed this as a possible future career path. They've all been teachers at some point, but some have left the 'chalkface' quite quickly and lack up to date experience. It's one of the criticisms of the teaching system; some of the best practitioners are promoted out of the classroom. They also, rather like Governors, have to tread that fine line of being the 'critical friend' of the headteacher-challenging them to keep developing the school, but showing practical support when the going gets tough, as it inevitably will at some point or other. Mo is responsible for about fifteen schools, so I suppose perhaps the skill is working out whereabouts on the 'support/ challenge' fine line each of her heads are at any given moment.

Advisers are not only involved in meetings such as these but also run a comprehensive programme of training throughout the county and are often also to be found on interview panels for senior positions. Some of their feedback has been useful to me in the past when I've been unsuccessful on interview days; some of it less so. I remember one chap a few years ago said to me, "you could perhaps try and make your accent a bit less Southeast London and a bit more Northwest Kent." I think it was half said in jest, but I was a bit non-plussed by that. Regional accents shouldn't really come into it, should they? The irony was the headteacher of that school was, I happened to know, Bolton born and bred. Lovely fellah, great teacher and head, but certainly didn't speak with a plumb in his mouth.

How easy is it to modify your natural accent, especially when you're nervous, anyway? I found myself thinking back to a story my Dad used to tell about his schooling in Catford (Southeast London!) in the immediate post-war years. Apparently, their form teacher was also the French master and insisted every morning on the class answering the register not with the traditional 'yes, sir', but with their number on the register, in French. Roffey, the poor unfortunate who was thirty-one in the register, would reply with a 'tren-a-un' full of glottal stops that would incite the ire of Mr Smith on a daily basis. Dad often had us roaring with laughter at his reenactments of this classroom scene.

Anyway, back in our meeting with Mo, we look carefully at our Y6 children and in the three core subjects of Maths, English and Science haggle over what percentage of them can reasonably be expected to achieve the expected Level 4, and how many might reach the dizzy heights of Level 5. The problem is that Mo herself is under pressure to get her schools to agree to targets that are as high as possible. Hertfordshire is widely regarded, not unfairly, as one of the most affluent and potentially high achieving areas in the country, and Tring is seen, again not without justification, as one of the most affluent and potentially high achieving parts of the county. So, the very lowest target we could get away with is somewhere in the region of 75%. We have around sixty children in Year Six, so one child is worth nearly 2% on their own. If ten of your sixty don't achieve Level 4, that's 83%.

We've done our homework prior to the meeting, and are able to point to a number of SEN issues and other matters that Mo is happy to concede might realistically mean pupil X, Y or Z falling short. In return, we find ourselves having to give ground in terms of higher Level 5 targets than we're comfortable with.

With that part of the meeting over, we then move on to look in detail at last May's results. What do they imply around the relative achievements in the three different subjects? What about how boys did in comparison to girls? What about children with and without English as an additional language? Children on free school meals compared to those that aren't? Children on the SEN register compared to those that aren't? There's a lot to think about and Mo both questions our methods and offers some ideas to think about how we might tweak them.

As she leaves, she promises a written report by the end of next week, and Brian and I are left discussing the merits of the suggested tweaks and which ones we might reasonably be suggesting (or even perhaps insisting on) at the next staff meeting. Brian tries to foster a "we're all in this together" culture, but inevitably a lot of the responsibility for the results fall on the shoulders of the two Year 6 teachers. This year, that doesn't include me. We had planned for me to be a 'floating' deputy this year, having more time out of the classroom to concentrate on whole school initiatives, and providing regular cover for each teacher every other week. But, our plans were scuppered with a late and unexpected resignation, so I'm now teaching a Year 5 class. I do enjoy Y5; they're old enough to get most of my jokes but I don't have to be worried quite so much (with them at least) about SATs, target setting and the like.

Chapter 16

A Varied Agenda.

Thursday, 11th October 2001

Thursday mornings are usually very early starts as I need to get my classroom all set up and my lessons for the day clear in my head before 8am. This is because 8am on a Thursday is the appointed hour for our weekly Senior Management meetings- that's Brian, me and Janet, our Senior Teacher. We've played around with the timing of these meetings, as we did at my other schools too; sometimes they've been after school, but people were tired then, and there was a danger they would drag on as there wasn't necessarily a clear 'cut off' time. With two of us needed in class at 8.55am, these meetings have a certain crispness to them.

We use these sessions for discussions on all aspects of school life; usually the School Development Plan and the current priorities for improving the school will form the basis for what we're talking about, but sometimes it's a more reactive agenda depending on what has happened in school since the last meeting.

Today there's lots to discuss. Top of our list is a challenging pupil who has already been suspended from school for a short time on a couple of occasions and is in danger of being permanently excluded. We thrash out a possible 'part time timetable' which we think might work over the next few weeks, and Brian will now make contact with the parents and seek their agreement. A 'part time timetable' is used very rarely as a way of managing a child's reintegration to a school, for example after suspension or illness. It is only ever a short-term solution and would be frowned upon by the LEA (Local Education Authority) and the DFE (Department for Education) if used for more than a few weeks.

We also talk about our provision for the Gifted and Talented children in our school. This is one of the current 'hot topics' in education, and from next year we are going to need to have in place a policy for how we propose to make sure our more able children are stretched. The thinking is that just as under Equal Opportunities legislation you make sure children who struggle with their learning have appropriate support in place, you need to stretch these children academically in order to give them a fair chance of reaching their potential. We talk about ways of enriching the curriculum and how these children could be recognised for their abilities.

Next, we move onto something that has been discussed in several Governors meetings lately: class splitting. This is the 'jumbling up' of pupils in a year group at the end of an academic year to create new classes for the following year. This is a process that had apparently been carried out regularly at Bishop Wood up until recently, but then a few years ago was done poorly one year and led to a lot of parental complaints, so it hasn't happened recently. Brian is interested to know our views on potentially bringing it back from next summer.

My own view is very pro this idea, and I even find myself offering to lead the process. I think it provides a new start for pupils each September and generally a calm start to the new academic year. It could also be used to separate children who do not work well together into different classes (although you might of course create new unhealthy alliances!) More importantly, it gives children the chance to experience getting to know new children and- perhaps- learning to live without having a particular close friend in their class. This might seem a bit callous (certainly there is a danger that some parents will look at it this way), but I believe it's really good preparation for secondary school, when there's every possibility this will happen, even when the vast majority of our pupils now transfer again to the same school (Tring does have its own secondary school, known, appropriately enough, as Tring School; it has an excellent reputation and caters for over 1000 students from the town and the surrounding villages.)

We finish our meeting with a few quick items: how can we support our MSAs (Midday Supervisory Assistants) some of whom are having a tough time, more effectively? What are our staff meetings going to be about after half term? What do we think of OFSTED's new consultation document? With unfinished conversations about all these ringing in my ears, I head off expectantly to the classroom ready for another day with 5H.

Chapter 17

Balancing Budgets and Fixing Leaky Roofs.

Friday, 11th October 2002

As I'm now a Deputy Head, I'm expected to attend all Governors meetings. And there's quite a few- four every half term to be precise. There are about fifteen governors altogether, and because we're a church school, a majority of them have to be Foundation Governors, which means they're appointed by the church. The remainder are the Headteacher, two Staff Governors (one teaching, one non-teaching), Parent Governors and one appointed by the LEA. Each half term the whole Governing Body meets together once. This is usually a meeting lasting around two hours on a weekday evening and starting at 8pm. There are three different committees that feed into the work of the Governors- the Curriculum, Finance and Personnel Committees. These happen earlier on weekday evenings, or in the case of the Personnel Committee, before school one morning. Fairly early on in my time here, I offered to take the minutes of the meetings, and although this adds to my workload, I find it a genuinely useful way of making sure I'm switched on in the meetings and focussed on the jobs that need doing once I've written them up.

The different committees hold a different level of interest for me. I enjoy the Curriculum Committee and its efforts to improve the teaching and learning in the school. I'm also keen on the Personnel Committee and its discussions around improving our workforce and how the school can support it. Finance is less of a turn on, though. It covers aspects of school life such as fixing leaky roofs (of which we have several) and balancing budgets; neither of these are reasons I went to teacher training college. I find the minutiae of these meetings quite hard to follow and understand at times, and even after I've asked for clarification several times, I'm aware that my minutes for these meetings are not quite as sharp as I like to think they are for the others. Nevertheless, I do acknowledge that roof maintenance and budget balancing have to be done, and if I have designs on becoming a Headteacher myself one day (the jury's still out on that at the moment), these are things I've got to try and get my head round.

Friday might seem an odd day for an after-school meeting, but things move along quickly and purposefully as the attendees are keen to get away and get on with their weekends. As ever, a number of issues are up for discussion today.

The Governors are keen to support our efforts to create a good 'Home-School Agreement' document. This has been a requirement of all schools for a few years now and sets out the responsibilities of the school, the parents and the pupils. The idea is that this is shared with new parents and the pupils when they enter the school in Year 3 and used as a sort of contract as they move through their four years with us. Parents, children and class teachers (on behalf of the school) sign to say they will do their best to carry out the requirements listed in the agreement. So, if a parent is not supporting the school in terms of ensuring their child is wearing the correct uniform, or getting homework done regularly, we can raise it with them. If a child is regularly misbehaving, we can point to the fact that they've signed up to say they will not do this. Equally, if the school is not providing a broad and balanced curriculum, or not maintaining a safe and happy environment, we can be held to account by the parents. I doubt the Agreement will ever help us solve major challenges, but it undoubtedly provides a useful framework to share expectations and remind ourselves of our responsibilities. An interesting discussion develops and a few tweaks to the current wording are agreed ready for next year's version.

Teacher workload is another hot topic and, again, this is an area that the Governors are interested to hear about our attempts to help the staff with. There is no doubt that expectations on teachers have increased enormously since I started teaching; the National Curriculum, the rise of OFSTED and the introduction of SATs have all played their part in creating an atmosphere of much greater public scrutiny. It seems generally accepted, therefore, that schools need to find ways of managing teacher workload and stress.

One way we have been trying to do this is through the introduction of 'Low Key Week.' This happens termly, and during that week, there are no after school meetings, you can cancel your after-school clubs (I tend to stick with my football club because it helps reduce rather than increase my stress levels), and you're encouraged to set tasks that involve little or no marking and leave school as near to 3.30pm as possible. I report to the meeting that this has gone down well with staff, and we discuss the feasibility of trying to do it every half term rather than just every term. This is an initiative which should help us with our upcoming 'Investors in People' re-recognition application. The school has been in receipt of an IIP accreditation since before I arrived. IIP organisations try to put their employees first and make work better for them. We will shortly be assessed to see if we can retain this status and the 'Low Key Week' idea should help.

We finish the meeting by reviewing where we are with the School Development Plan, talking about protocols around Governor visits to classrooms, and what we might include on our proposed new school website. There's a lot to think about as I head off home for my weekend.

Chapter 18

Headship: Thanks, but no Thanks!

Tuesday, 21st October 2003

This afternoon, it's back to Wheathampstead for a Headteacher's update. I am attending because this year I am officially the Acting Headteacher of the school. Unfortunately, for the last couple of years, Brian has suffered a period of ill health, and he has had increasingly lengthy periods of time out of school. I have had some really challenging times during which I have been both teaching and trying to run the school but have also had great support from Governors and they have ensured I've been able to be out of the classroom when it's been known Brian will be absent for an extended period. For large parts of the academic year 2001/02, my class was covered by Liz, a GTP (Graduate Teacher Programme- this is a new way of trainee teachers with a degree learning 'on the job') student and during 2002/03 by Nikki, a teacher from New Zealand. In both cases, we've been able to keep the school's financial head above water because they were both paid less than a fully qualified UK teacher would have been. The Governors have also been a real source of practical help to me as well; our previous Chair of Governors, Mike, took a day off work at the drop of a hat last term to help me with a crisis over the school reports, and his successor Sarah is fast turning into my surrogate mother, such is the depth of her day to day support of me.

The teachers have also rallied round and been really supportive of me. Janet is now on maternity leave, so I have Liz (not the GTP lady, but my Y6 partner from my first year here) as my Acting Deputy and Rosemary as my Acting Senior Teacher; both of them help me to keep my sanity when the going gets tough! The LEA must have considered looking around for someone else they could parachute in to be our

Acting Head, but instead, partly as a result, I think, of senior staff and Governors speaking up for me, I was given the go ahead to hold the fort. Mo has helped to arrange Kathy, an experienced and respected local Head, to come in and help mentor me in a series of fortnightly meetings. She has been great, and I've really benefitted from her expertise.

To say I have been out of my comfort zone would, however, be a massive understatement! I have enjoyed aspects of the job and I'm sure the whole experience has in some ways made me a tougher and more resilient person. I like most of the stuff to do with people; building a team and recruiting teachers and support staff, and helping pupils and their parents through difficulties. Sometimes, a parent has come into my office very angry about something and half an hour later has left much happier that we have a plan in place to try and improve the situation. Although, to be honest, this hasn't always been the case and dealing with very difficult parents is not a strength because I'm someone who naturally shies away from conflict. I've enjoyed the public speaking part of the role and am perfectly comfortable taking assemblies in front of the children and speaking to groups of parents at events and meetings. They say many teachers are just frustrated actors and I have to admit that, to some extent, I like showing off and being the centre of attention. I suppose I quite like, at times, the status of being in charge, too.

One of the key tasks of a Head, it seems to me, is to make a decision about each piece of paper that comes across your desk. There are quite a few pieces of paper most days. You have to decide to either a) do something about it yourself b) give it to someone else to do something about or c) file it in the bin. I've slowly been getting better at making the a, b or c decisions, but sometimes it's quite scary when you're sitting there on your own and you genuinely don't know whether something is an a, b or c. Overall, though, I've quite enjoyed learning this skill.

The finance and premises aspects of the job, however, continue to baffle me, and without the safety nets of our brilliant Finance Governor Karin and Brian's willingness to help from the other end of a phone line, I think I'd have gone mad by now! How are you supposed to understand all this stuff?! I suppose the honest answer is to enrol on a NPQH course. This relatively new course is the National Professional Qualification for Headship. I attended a taster session for this a couple of years ago and it seemed to me like doing another degree whilst holding down a full-time job, so I politely declined the opportunity to take it on.

This afternoon's meeting is a chance to meet with other Hertfordshire heads and swap strategies for dealing with the complexities of the job, and also to receive an update on current issues from some of the LEA advisers. It certainly does me good to hear that even some very experienced heads are tearing their hair out at times. We listen to some updated information on the National Literacy Strategy, and on how to implement the Tackling Workload National Agreement (a list of 25 tasks that teachers should not routinely be undertaking has recently been published; these include bulk photocopying, collecting money and chasing absences.)

Brian has recently decided that he is going to retire permanently at the end of this academic year. I have been asked for some time now by my colleagues, by parents and by Governors if I am interested in applying for the permanent headship. I love the school, and the parents and pupils are generally very supportive of what we're trying to do, but I have decided against it. Overall, I've found the job a bit too much for me; I feel lucky that I've had a chance to see what it's like to have your 'name over door', but can now withdraw gracefully and say 'thanks but no thanks.'

It's brought me a great deal of pressure and anxiety. I've probably tried to do too much myself and have learnt that I'm not a great delegator. I've almost certainly spent too much time shut away in the Head's office and not enough time out in the school with the children and staff. This has reinforced in my mind that headship is a very lonely job, but perhaps if I'd approached it differently it wouldn't have felt that way. In terms of applying for the job permanently, I know I'd trip up on the 'vision' aspect of the role. I'm not a Doug, my previous Head, who had a very clear idea of where his school was going and where he wanted it to be in a year's time, in three years' time, and so on. I'm much better at implementing a vision- one of life's lieutenants, perhaps.

I am also aware that I've taken the job home far too much and found it very hard to 'switch off.' I've not been easy for Sandra, my new partner, to live with. I've been prescribed anti-depressants by my doctor, and they've calmed me to the extent that I think I'll be able to see this through to the summer now. Interviews for the new Head are now on the horizon. Of course, there is a possibility that I will find the new postholder difficult to work with, and will have to move on to pastures new, but time will tell on that one.

Chapter 19

Disneyland, David Beckham and
a Roller Hockey pitch.

Friday, October 8th 2004

Fortunately for me, I am now back as a plain old Deputy Headteacher. It turns out that, unsurprisingly, I was not alone in not being keen on headship, and it proved quite tricky to recruit a new one. When the job was first advertised, the Governors felt that none of the applicants warranted an interview. I didn't of course see the applications, but secretly was frustrated by this, as it raised the possibility of me staying as Acting Head beyond last summer.

However, mercifully, a second advert later in the year yielded a more promising field, and my new boss, Linda, emerged from the process. It is, of course, early days in our working relationship, but the signs are good- Linda is a 'people person' and she is already imposing her calm and considered leadership on us, without making the fatal mistake of making changes for changes sake.

Last academic year was hugely challenging given that it included an OFSTED inspection in May. I could have wept when we were informed of this two months previously, but I was half expecting it, as the school had not been inspected since the summer of 1999, the term before I arrived. However, once again I received fantastic support from staff, Governors and Mo (who at one point stepped out of a family party to talk to me on the phone for 40 minutes whilst I completed a vital piece of pre-inspection documentation), and somehow, we got through it with all aspects of the school judged at least 'satisfactory' and many of them deemed 'good.' Much of our work in school at the moment is to do with implementing our OFSTED Action Plan, which all schools are required to draw up after an inspection.

Anyway, today I am back doing something I really enjoy, sitting in on the second School Council meeting of the new academic year. Our School Council is a group of pupils who meet each Friday lunchtime to discuss school issues and try and help improve the school.

At Bishop Wood, we have sixteen School Council members; that's two from each class. We try and have one boy and one girl from each class, although that is not strictly enforced. I come along as an observer, but I do not run the meetings. We attempt to make sure that you are only a School Councillor once in your time at Bishop Wood, and the membership changes termly. So, in theory, most children (24/30) can have a go at being a School Councillor during their time at the school, if they want to.

At the start of each term, each class has a vote to elect their school councillors for that term. I give my class a little pep-talk about what it involves, and sternly remark that if they're elected they must make sure they attend all meetings, and not conveniently forget and stay out on the playground or field during the lunchtime meetings (this tends to be more of a problem in the summer term when the weather is good and a kick about with your mates is more attractive than being sat in a classroom moaning about the school dinners!) I like to take these votes seriously; candidates are banished to the dining hall (if possible, under the watchful eye of a Teaching Assistant!) and voters have to shut their eyes, put their heads on the desks and raise their hands when the name of the person they want to vote for is read out. If I've got the time and energy, I explain a bit about electoral history, the Secret Ballot Act of 1872 and what the problems around everybody else knowing how you voted were.

At the first meeting of each term, this process is repeated amongst the sixteen councillors to choose a Chairperson and a Secretary for the term. From week two, the Chairperson runs the meetings and the Secretary types up the minutes, which I then usually polish before distribution to the classes. The quality of the work of the Council is largely dependent on the skills of the two people elected to these roles.

Occasionally, I have inwardly groaned when realising that someone who is going to struggle to keep order or type coherently has been chosen, but with some guidance all children can to some extent grow into the jobs after a few weeks, and they definitely learn a lot from the process, which is part of the reason for the School Council in the first place.

The discussions are always interesting. Similar topics of course come up most years. Today's main job is to choose which charity the school is going to support for the academic year. We have several events across the year when money is raised for charity, and the School Council gets to choose which one it will be.

The most eagerly awaited of these events by the children (and at least some of the staff) is the Lenten Bazaar, which takes place towards the end of the Spring Term. This event has been running at Bishop Wood since around the time that Brian became Head in 1987, and is often remarked upon by returning pupils and parents. The children, completely in their own time, at home, design a game of some sort, which they then bring into school on the appointed day. All the games are set up in the school hall, then the children go around playing each other's games. A small charge is made to play, and all games come with prizes (generally sweets or chocolates.) The atmosphere is joyful, chaotic and extremely noisy. Most adults can take about twenty minutes max before decamping to the dining room and the sanctuary of the tea and coffee bar. At the end of the bazaar, all the takings from each stall are emptied into some receptacle or other and carried to the school office for counting. There's usually the odd Year 3 child or two who is extremely disgruntled to learn they cannot keep the money for themselves.

Back in today's School Council meeting, there are lots of different charity nominations that the children have brought from their classes, and after a lively discussion and a vote, they choose the Guide Dogs for the Blind Association.

Often in these meetings, another subject for discussion is the school dinners and how they can be improved. The cook always accepts the notes from these discussions graciously and takes them to her meetings with our lunch providers, Herts Catering. Although occasionally she can implement a suggestion, I have to explain to the children that she is working to a budget and some of their ideas are just not possible from a financial point of view. This applies to other issues too- school trips to Disneyland, a visit from David Beckham and a new roller hockey pitch on the lower playground have all recently found their way into the School Council suggestion box but been dismissed because the school is not bankrolled by Bill Gates. It's good to hear some of the older pupils pointing this out to their younger counterparts.

Sometimes, though, the Council does have an impact on school life. Last term, the poor decorative state of the Year 6 toilets was raised at the meetings. These toilets are the only ones in the school outside the actual classrooms and had certainly become a bit rundown and shabby looking. We were able to organise a couple of after-school painting sessions, and School Council members came along and helped spruce them up. There was some good learning around choice of colours and pricing, and even though the caretaker and I had to do some subtle tidying up of their painting efforts, it was definitely a worthwhile exercise.

We also regularly talk about new suggestions for 'Golden Time' activities. 'Golden Time' is a common phenomenon in primary schools and is part of our behaviour policy. For the last hour on a Friday afternoon, teachers offer a 'Golden Time' activity that children from any class in the school can sign up for. I tend to offer some sort of quiz or sporting activity, typically cross country round the school grounds in the winter and non-stop cricket in the summer. Other more creative members of staff will offer arty type activities, and there might also be a video of some sort on offer. It is assumed that all children will take part in this session, but a portion of the hour (or in extreme cases the whole thing) can be removed for poor behaviour. It seems to work well and the majority of children, particularly in the lower years (I'm now in Year 4), will soon knuckle down to their work if the removal of ten minutes of Golden Time is threatened.

The meeting ends five minutes before the end of lunch hour, so I have time for a quick check of the Secretary's notes and a few changes to her generally very good set of minutes before 4H come marauding through the door ready for afternoon lessons.

Chapter 20

A Reserved Englishman learns
how to Give Out Praise.

Monday, 10th October 2005

Today, I am meeting my colleague Richard after school for his Performance Management interview. A few years ago, in 2002, another Education Act led to an important change in schools. Amongst other things, it required by law all schools to undertake an annual performance review of all teachers. At the time, some of us were rather sceptical about yet another initiative which smacked of big business and the private sector rather than something that would be particularly useful in schools. Nevertheless, the government argued that this would improve the quality of education by giving teachers a chance to reflect on their performance and identify training opportunities where there was a need for improvement. This felt to some like yet another layer of accountability and, crucially, it could for many people be related to their pay; if a movement up the pay scales was in the offing, it would now be subject to successfully meeting targets set in a performance management interview.

Despite these misgivings, the process has quickly become established in schools and each year, around this time, we review last year's targets for each teacher and whether they've been achieved, and then re-start the process by setting some targets for the current year. These targets need to be related to the school's priorities for development and they will be assessed partly through classroom observations. The Governors have oversight of this process and will expect some general (though not person specific) feedback in meetings.

Linda has responsibility for setting and reviewing my objectives, but as her Deputy I have the task of leading the performance management of some of my colleagues- hence this afternoon's meeting with Richard. It's really important that this is done in a professional and respectful way. Partly because of my recent experience as Acting Head, I have a pretty good knowledge of my colleagues' strengths and areas for development anyway, and I believe all of them to be competent teachers, so I have no major worries about having to have very difficult conversations. Richard has been with us a few years and we swapped year groups this year, he moving to Year 4, and me back once again where I started at Bishop Wood, in Year 6.

When I am setting Performance Management Objectives with teachers, I always try to be positive and begin the discussions with plenty of praise for their work around school. It's interesting to observe their reaction to this; I'm not sure the English as a race are very good at accepting (or indeed giving out) praise, and teachers as a profession certainly aren't; I've noticed over the years a definite tendency to brush it off and play it down. I include myself in all this. Carol, the Deputy at Fair Field, was American and effusive in her praise of all her colleagues on a regular basis. I found it quite uncomfortable at first, but came to realise that in fact she was just being positive, supportive and downright nice, and that this reserved Englishman had more than a little to learn from her approach.

Once I've finished with all the praise, we move onto the potentially more difficult part of the interview- the areas for development. The key here is to have done a bit of preparation prior to the meeting. I always ask my appraisees to have a think beforehand about what their targets could be, and I always do some thinking before my meeting about areas I'd like to develop. Then, when I ask, or am asked, "have you got any ideas about what your targets might be for this year?" there hopefully won't be a deafening silence.

Richard and I agree that his targets for last year have been met and set some new ones related to his classroom practice and his stewardship of PE. We browse the list of upcoming courses provided by the LEA and enrol him on a couple that will hopefully help him to achieve the objectives we've set. As an experienced teacher, he is at the top of his scale, and so his pay will not be affected either way.

I reflect that as I'm now entering my seventh year as a Deputy Head, I too have reached as high as I can go salary wise unless I move to a different school with a higher upper salary limit, or unless the Governors choose to increase ours. Currently, as far as I can tell from my still less than perfect grasp of the Governors Finance Committee meetings, the school is in a relatively healthy financial position, so that is not beyond the bounds of possibility, but otherwise any future increases will come down to the annual salary shenanigans conducted between the government and the teaching unions.

Still, pay increases notwithstanding, professional pride will drive me on, and as I bid farewell to Richard, my mind turns towards my own Performance Management Interview with Linda next week and my ideas for my own targets for the coming year.

Chapter 21

Autumn Days.

Monday, October 9th 2006

One aspect of being a Deputy Head that I generally like is taking assemblies. As a Church of England school, we take our legal duty to provide for the children a daily Act of Worship very seriously, and it is highly unusual for it not to happen. Every day, currently between the first block of the teaching day and morning break, we meet as a whole school in our beautiful hall. The children are arranged in a sort of straight-sided horseshoe shape around the room, with classes sitting together in blocks. The theory is that this is a bit more inclusive and welcoming of everybody rather than just sitting in rows.

There are lots of different types of assembly. It could be the Headteacher or the Deputy taking an assembly on a particular theme (we try to follow a plan drawn up at the start of the term, but are also flexible and will include world, national or school events as appropriate.)

It could be that Frank, the vicar of St Peter and St Paul's church across the road, comes in to talk to the children; he does this most weeks. We also, on a more occasional basis, invite church leaders from other denominations in to lead an assembly.

It might be a hymn and singing practice taken by Susan, our music teacher. We took Susan on as a specialist music teacher a few years ago. Many of us class teachers were delighted by this, because it means that we don't have to teach music, a subject notoriously difficult for the non-specialist, to our own classes. Susan now has the unenviable task of teaching all eight of our classes for half an hour or so every Monday up in the Music Room (a room separate from the rest of the school which was converted from the changing rooms for the old swimming pool which no longer exists.)

It could be a Celebration Assembly in which certificates for good work in class are given out and children get to bring in certificates, trophies or medals for achievements outside school. I usually get to preside over these, and they're good fun.

I'm also the go to person for an emergency assembly if the headteacher or visitor can't take the assembly at the last minute. On a number of occasions, I've been most grateful for Doug's farewell present when I left Fair Field, which was a book of assembly stories. I have some special favourites from within this trusty tome, and the staff tease me that they've heard several of them a number of times. I do try and keep a record of what stories I use and when, but none of the children seem to mind too much if they've heard a story before-perhaps they have short memories or are off in their own little worlds while I'm reading, not actually listening at all!

Sometimes, we invite parents in to watch an assembly led by a class. This will usually focus on an aspect of their work that they've been covering in class but will still contain a religious element with a prayer and hymn at least. We try to involve every child in the class in these, and it takes a lot of time to put them together; the normal timetable is essentially put to one side in the week running up to the assembly, and there's lots of delicate staff room negotiations about getting in the hall when someone else is supposed to be doing PE in order to practice.

Today, we are combining several of these types of assembly and hosting the Harvest Festival in school. Frank leads the service, the children bring in different tinned and non-perishable foodstuffs for distribution to the local elderly and needy, each year group performs a poem or song, and we sing some harvest hymns, including my favourite *Autumn Days*. Some would say this is a strange choice as a favourite hymn; I have a vague recollection of a news item about some choristers walking out of a service some years ago and refusing to sing it because of some complaint about the lyrics. However, I love the simplicity of the message around all the autumnal things we should thank God for, and the children always sing it with gusto, especially the last line of the last verse, "and a win for my home team!" which is invariably shouted rather than sung.

It's certainly a far cry from the more traditional *We Plough the Fields and Scatter,* which I loved as a child, but it goes down well with the assembled masses, and as the children and parents stream happily out of the hall, we can cross the Harvest Festival off the jobs list for another year.

Chapter 22

"Fun, Fit and Fruity Week."

Monday, 7th October 2007

This morning is an early start because we are expecting around fifty children on the school field at 8.15am for a Cross-Country run. This is the first event in what is fast becoming a tradition around this time of year, "Fun, Fit and Fruity Week." This is a week where we at least partly suspend normal lessons and focus on learning about different aspects of a healthy lifestyle. Today also marks the start of one of our regular "Low Key Weeks", with no after school meetings and marking-free classroom activities encouraged, so it provides a refreshing change for staff and pupils alike.

I love weeks like this in school; you can let your hair down a bit (although eight years into Deputy Headship, the amount of actual hair I have left is declining rapidly, and the colour of that which still remains is taking on an increasingly grey tinge), take things a little less seriously and you get to see some of the children in a different light. Someone who struggles with fractions or punctuation might be more inspired by a greater number of lessons on the field or in the hall.

My indefatigable colleague Janet is now back with us after a second maternity leave and is leading our work to do with the government's National Healthy Schools Programme (NHSP), which was launched around the turn of the century. This programme covers healthy eating, physical activity, alcohol and drug awareness, sex education and emotional well-being. Although some of this is covered in PSHE and PE lessons, we use "Fun, Fit and Fruity Week" to enrich the learning in these aspects of the curriculum, in particular by inviting a range of visitors into school.

Janet has built up an impressive list of contacts over the last few years and each year group will have at least one 'special' activity per day. During "Fun, Fit and Fruity Week", we have had fitness coaches, dance instructors, yoga and meditation teachers, skipping workshops, golf professionals, cycling proficiency instructors and others in school to work with the children.

As well as visitors, other events take place too. Some of the older children, known as Sports Ambassadors, teach some of the younger ones some new playground games at playtime and lunchtime. Each year group has a day in the week when they're allowed to ride their bikes on certain parts of the field at lunchtime. I get a bit jumpy about this if the weather is wet as I don't want the bikes to damage the football pitch. Each year group is also invited to do some cooking or food related creativity at home on a particular theme- for example pizzas, smoothies, salads or healthy snack bars. On a given day, they bring in their creations and some judges from another year group will test their creations and mark them out of ten according to certain criteria, with prizes for the winners.

We also try and have a big push on encouraging 'active travel' to school this week. This means walking, cycling or scooting to school if at all possible. Like most schools, drop off and pick up times can be pretty congested around our site. Lives are busy and some parents have little choice but to use the car to drop their children before dashing off to work, but we try and encourage 'Park and Stride', an initiative where children are dropped off away from the school and then walk the last bit; this not only allows the children to have a partly active journey, but reduces road danger around our school gates.

Janet even encourages the staff to ditch the cars during this week and the national "Walk to School Week", which tends to take place in May. One year I got up at some ungodly hour and cycled to Tring from my home in Hemel Hempstead. This is a distance of about ten miles or so, and I used the canal towpath rather than run the gauntlet of the busy A41. I quite enjoyed the outward journey, and, despite arriving at work rather more sweaty than usual, I felt energised for most of the day. But the return journey in the evening was a slog, my backside ached for days after and the following year, I politely declined to participate.

The cross-country run is as well attended as the sign-up sheet suggested it would be. Janet leads some stretching exercises first, then I lead the children round the course in a slow jog warm up lap, in which nobody is allowed to overtake me. Once that is complete, the children are challenged to see how many further laps of the course they can complete in the half hour or so now remaining before the start of school. I jog a few more laps and then rest to drink some coffee that a kind colleague has brought me from the staff room. The children, with their boundless energy, keep going and seem to enjoy this unusual start to a working week, even if some of them find it impossible to keep an accurate tally of the number of laps they have completed, and hugely exaggerate their totals to their friends!

Chapter 23

Staying positive and 'taking it on the chin.'

Thursday, 2nd October 2008

Tonight, at Governors, we are dissecting last week's OFSTED inspection, the third one of my career, and starting to formulate our Action Plan to address the areas for improvement. The report is not yet formally published (indeed the school is not allowed to communicate the findings to the parents at this stage), but the Lead Inspector gave us thorough feedback at the end of the inspection, and we already know what the report will be saying.

The main difference between this inspection and previous ones that I have experienced was the notice period given beforehand. Due to recent changes in the inspection framework, schools are now only given 48 hours warning of an OFSTED visit, compared to many months in the past.

It is easy to see why the general public would consider this a better system- no chance for a school to spend weeks on end getting policies, systems and displays in place and therefore a much more accurate picture of what a school is really like. However, for those of us at the sharp end, it's a little less than convenient. We got the call a week last Tuesday for an inspection on the Thursday. I had a prior evening commitment with my beloved Arsenal on the Tuesday evening, so could not help with the last-minute preparations as much as I would've liked. I considered selling my ticket or simply not going, but in the end decided that going to the game would probably keep me more relaxed and able to do my best on the day rather than just spending a long evening in school.

The day itself was extremely full on and intense. The inspector was once again thorough, business-like and extremely intelligent. These people are very well trained and do not miss a trick. The result of the inspection was that all areas looked at were again deemed either 'Good' or 'Satisfactory', but that the overall effectiveness of the school was only 'Satisfactory.' To say that we feel a little deflated by this is an understatement. I feel particularly for Linda, who has, we all think, moved the school forward markedly in the last four years, but on paper she has nothing to show for that. We get individual feedback on our own lessons as well, and mine was considered only satisfactory too, with the inspector feeling I 'spoon-fed' the class too much, and did more work than the children, with she taking the view that it should be the other way round.

The atmosphere in tonight's Governors' meeting is a muted one. Governors too are part of the inspection, and their role also elicited mixed reviews in the feedback. My emotions flit between a deep frustration, depression and even anger that all our hard work can be damned with such faint praise as 'satisfactory' to a fiery 'we'll fix this and blooming well show them' type of resolve.

We have to try and not take things personally. The inspector, I am certain, has made her judgements in good faith and with the well-being and best interests of the pupils at heart. So, hard as it is, we have to take this on the chin and find a way to move forward.

In summary, we did very well on the personal development and care of the children, but less well on maximising academic potential. So, our discussions this evening focus on ways of improving the latter, without losing the former. A difficult balance to strike. Schools should be about producing well rounded, thoughtful pupils as well as simply instilling knowledge and skills. But it seems perhaps we haven't been rigorous enough with this second task; to some extent this is the view of the pupils and parents too as their opinions were also sought and form part of the final report.

So, we will need to up our game. We decide that we need to look carefully at how our 'Booster Classes' for those children who might not achieve the required standard in their SATs are organised. More widely, I am tasked with undertaking a review of all Interventions that currently take place in the school. An Intervention is an activity, usually run by a Teaching Assistant, that supports a small group of children with a particular activity, such as spelling. I will find out exactly what interventions are happening, who is in them, for how long, and how the impact of them is evaluated. I promise to report back to the next Governors' Curriculum Committee.

We also agree that closer and more regular monitoring of progress in every class in the core subjects will be done through 'Pupil Progress Meetings'; these will happen termly and be my responsibility in Maths, as I am the current co-ordinator. It is agreed that our assessment systems need looking at, and that the Senior Leadership Team (me again) will need to observe teachers more regularly.

On several occasions, I shift slightly uncomfortably in my seat; the report has clearly identified Maths as the weak link of the three core subjects, and that's my baby. I agree to make contact with the County Maths adviser for some help on maths investigations, and to set up a Numeracy Evening for parents to talk to them about current methods so that they're better able to support their children with their learning.

So, in the end a worthwhile meeting with lots of ideas put forward to help us tackle the issues raised. One of the challenges going forward will be to make sure that I stay positive about all of this in front of the staff; even on the days when those feelings of frustration, depression and anger are there, I cannot afford to show them. Part of my job is to stay upbeat and encourage them that this Action Plan is realistic and doable!

Chapter 24

The Secret Angel(s).

Monday, 12th October 2009

That time of year has come around again. Today marks the start of another Fun, Fit and Fruity Week. It's again been made a 'Low-Key Week', and this year we have added an extra dimension- 'The Secret Angel.' This is another idea aimed at improving the wellbeing of the staff. It's sort of a variation on the 'Secret Santa' idea used at Christmas. During the past fortnight, each staff member has drawn the name of a colleague out of a hat. Twice this week, the plan is that we will leave a compliment and a little gift on the desk of or in the pigeonhole of whoever we have drawn. So, the person doing the gifting and complimenting is acting as 'The Secret Angel' of the recipient.

I reflect that my own wellbeing was under serious attack earlier this year. During the Spring Term, I suffered what I am starting to see, given some distance from the event and sense of perspective, as a form of nervous breakdown. For those three desperately difficult months, I spent a lot more time out of school than I did in it, and I honestly felt on more than one occasion that my teaching career might be over.

I hadn't felt great for most of the Christmas holiday. Initially I just put this down to the usual end of term scenario of your mind and body relaxing and the germs moving in, but by the New Year, I was suffering from chest pain and anxiety. I made several panicked visits to the local Urgent Care Centre and my GP. Various tests revealed nothing of major concern, the cause of the pain was thought to be a hiatus hernia, and I was referred to the local hospital for further investigations.

Once the new term got underway, I tried to work through this and go into school, but teaching is not a job that can easily be sustained when your mind and body are not in the right place, and more than once I was out of school, went back, but then had to take further time off. The likely effects of all this on the children, my colleagues and the school bank balance (we have insurance to cover the cost of supply teachers, but that only kicks in on the third day of absence) only served to make me feel worse, mentally if not physically.

I knew things were bad when I was recognised by name at my local pharmacy! Under the guidance of my GP, I tweaked my blood pressure medication, and used painkillers and sleeping tablets to try and help the situation, before reluctantly submitting to anti-depressants for the second time in my life. I also joined a local meditation group and went back to a brilliant counsellor I had previously used for relationship support about five years ago.

By the end of that term, I was still not teaching full time, but able to go into school, catch up on some administrative tasks, and act as a Teaching Assistant in my class, supporting the work of the supply teacher. After Easter, as the anti-depressants started to do their thing, I felt a lot more relaxed, and was able to 'get back on the horse.' I was fully aware that without the caring and understanding of Linda, who was happy for me to take my time recovering and getting into the right headspace to resume full time work, I might have been forced to resign. Looking back, the patience and support of Sandra and my long-suffering parents was also vital. Those four between them took on the role of my 'Secret Angels.'

The 'Secret Angel' initiative is proving to be a worthwhile one. The atmosphere around school today is very positive; people that have already received a gift or a compliment are enjoying them, and those that haven't as yet are looking forward to doing so. I'm pleased to hear a lot of cheerful and upbeat chat in the staffroom.

So why did I succumb to all that anxiety and worry at that time? It's difficult to know whether the physical symptoms caused the mental ones, or if it was the other way round. With the benefit of hindsight, it does feel as though the stresses and strains of last Autumn's OFSTED inspection were certainly quite a big factor. Maths took a bit of a hammering, and I was the Co-ordinator. The SATs results and academic standards generally were criticised, and I as Deputy Head and one of the Year 6 teachers of course felt particularly responsible. Certainly, with regards to the Maths, I felt like I'd done an awful lot to try and improve things in the years leading up to that inspection, and clearly that hadn't worked. I was at a bit of a loss as to what else I could do.

Linda came up trumps again. We have a dynamic, reasonably new member of staff, Ruth, who was happy to take on Maths and Year 6 for this academic year. I have moved back to Year 4 and taken on History and Geography instead. Although still Deputy Head, I feel somewhat out of the firing line when it comes to implementing our Action Plan.

However, now my newly restored mental balance, and that of all my colleagues, is being threatened again. Last month, we were subject to a two-day mini-inspection by three LEA advisers. It was billed as a way of helping to turn our satisfactory school into a good one. To say this did not go as we'd hoped would be putting it mildly. On a personal note, two of my three lessons observed were rated 'inadequate'; most definitely not a word I wanted to hear after my travails earlier in the year.

But it wasn't just me. The advisers tore into us- the hour and a half's feedback was without doubt the most uncomfortable hour and a half of my career so far. We are now, as far as the LEA is concerned, a 'School Causing Concern', a dubious title which apparently up to 10% of schools in the authority can be saddled with at any one time.

What this means in practice is that an 'Action Group' consisting of Linda, one of the advisers and Jenny (our current Chair of Governors) will meet once a half term to first of all write, and then regularly review, another 'Action Plan.' Whether this completely usurps, or runs alongside, the 'Action Plan' we're still trying to implement from the OFSTED inspection, I'm not entirely clear about. I suspect it's the latter.

The main areas we have been tasked to improve are: differentiation, challenging our Gifted and Talented pupils, having higher expectations of all pupils, assessment and planning, questioning skills, Guided Reading, lesson objectives and success criteria, children's writing, plenaries and our modelling and demonstrating skills. The view of the advisers was that these skills do exist amongst some of our teachers, but they are not used consistently across all classes, so we need to get better at coaching each other.

It's another big challenge for us as a school. On a personal level, after that really difficult term earlier this year, I'm determined that I will keep things in perspective and not go under this time. But I might need my Secret Angels to help keep me afloat.

Chapter 25

The Carpet Salesman pays
a visit (in lieu of OFSTED.)

Monday, 11th October 2010

This afternoon, Linda is coming to watch my Shared Writing lesson with 4H. I am not too worried because I know Linda values my work in school, and she will put a positive spin on her feedback to me come what may. But this lesson observation forms part of a growing amount of 'monitoring' activities that are happening in school. School Self Evaluation, the process whereby we look at our own strengths and weaknesses as a school, and try to act on the latter, is a well-established part of school life and has been around in one form or another for the whole of my career.

The amount of monitoring undertaken, fuelled by our 'Satisfactory' and 'School Causing Concern' judgements, has, however, increased markedly over the last few years. As well as lesson observations, other activities include Pupil Progress Meetings, Book Scrutinies, Learning Walks and Planning File checks. The idea of all this is that when inspectors or advisers come calling, Linda, myself, other SLT members and indeed the Governors will know where the school is at and have plans in place to address any issues. We are being told that the cardinal sin now is to be unaware of problems that inspectors find.

A couple of months after last September's harrowing LEA mini-inspection, we were treated to an OFSTED 'monitoring visit.' This put us under a whole new level of pressure. The Government have now decreed that 'Satisfactory' schools will be given a twenty working day window in which these monitoring visits will be carried out; you get told when the window is, but not the actual days of the inspection; it could come on days one and two or days nineteen and twenty of the window. It is not clear which megalomaniac within OFSTED came up with this scheme, but if we ever found out, some of my colleagues and I might have some very strong words indeed for this warped individual.

Our window started in early November of last year. I have never known such collective stress in a school. Everybody was on a war footing, girding their loins for the visit and determined to show the school in a good light. Things descended into farce on about day four of the twenty day block, when the office staff received a garbled message on the school answerphone along the lines of "you'll know who I am, I'm just leaving Guildford now, see you in a couple of hours." Well, this was it. For the remainder of that day, every time my classroom door opened, I expected an inspector to walk in. But he (the voice had been male) never did. Eventually, it turned out that the person making the call had been a carpet salesman, visiting us to provide a quote to carpet one of the classrooms. With hindsight, this was of course hilarious, but at the time it just served to highlight the ridiculously stressful situation we were all trying to work under.

When the real inspector eventually arrived to put us out of our misery on approximately days sixteen and seventeen of our window, he proved to be very pleasant and fair. He acknowledged improvements in our English and Science results, found the majority of our teaching to be good, but due to our ongoing issues with Maths, and below average progress generally, was only able to rate our progress since the last inspection as satisfactory, with only a satisfactory capacity to improve further in the future. He explained we could expect another full inspection any time after November 2010, so we're nearly at that point now!

Crucially, from our point of view, he did acknowledge that "the system is not set up to be fair for junior schools." Schools are judged not only on the attainment of their pupils, but on their progress, or what has come to be known as the 'value added' to their academic level. Our feeder infant school always send us children with extremely high KS1 results. We have no control over these, but it means we have to get the children to extremely high levels four years later at KS2, just to show satisfactory (or expected) progress. To make good (or better than expected) progress in these circumstances is extremely challenging. In a whole-through primary school, headteachers can ask their KS1 teachers to suppress their reported levels a little, so that good levels of progress can be shown four years later. Of course, they would never admit to doing this, but the comment from the inspector confirmed for us that this is exactly what does happen. Huw, our new vicar (and therefore on our Governing Body) and I have written what we consider to be a carefully crafted letter to Michael Gove, the new Education Secretary, on this very matter. We are awaiting his reply with interest.

Anyway, back to all this monitoring. Formal lesson observations happen regularly, and every teacher can expect one each half term. It may be to focus on a particular aspect of the school's work, like this afternoon's one on Shared Writing, which is something the whole school is trying to get to grips with now. Best practice is to give the feedback within forty-eight hours at the most, while the lesson itself is still fresh in the mind of the observer and the observee. If I'm observing, I always try to accentuate the positives, and if at all possible, only give one target for improvement next time, ideally a target that we agree together having talked through the lesson, rather than one imposed by me. In a perfect world, that target should be checked on in the next observation, but the reality is that by then the agenda may have changed and we're now focussing on something entirely different making a check on that matter difficult.

In recent years, we have also begun what are known as 'Pupil Progress Meetings.' These happen termly and require some preparation by the class teacher. They must look at how the children in their class are doing in the three core subjects and fill out some paperwork to show what percentage of the class are at each level, and how quickly they're progressing. In the meeting itself, the Curriculum Co-ordinator and the Headteacher talk to the Class Teacher about any children who are not progressing as they should, and agree on some actions that might improve the situation. These may be interventions either inside or outside the classroom, and may involve parental input too. This is a way of focussing more assiduously on individual pupils who can hopefully improve our overall results at the end of KS2.

Book Scrutinies are another form of monitoring. These are carried out by Curriculum Co-ordinators with a view to getting a clear understanding of what is happening in their subjects. Typically, class teachers will be asked to provide six books, two from above average ability children, two from average ability children and two from below average ability children. The co-ordinator will then look at the books, checking on issues such as curriculum coverage, how the activities match to the planning, differentiation, presentation and so on. Individual feedback may be given, but more usually it is general feedback in staff meetings.

Another form of monitoring that is becoming popular is called a 'Learning Walk.' This is where an adviser or SLT member tours all the classrooms, looking at the same issue across the school, and spending just a short period of time (maybe ten minutes) in each room. The observers may look at behaviour, for example, or teacher questioning, or the use of display. This last issue has formed the basis for some of our recent 'Learning Walks.'

The use of display has certainly changed since I started teaching. Back in the Eighties, all display was children's work, and I remember trying to ensure that at least one piece of work from every child in the class was on the wall at any given time. Now, although some children's work is still up on the walls, much more wall space is taken up with information that'll help the pupils with their learning. So, worked examples of a particular type of maths problem, or useful vocabulary for a particular topic. I reckon I spend a lot less time on display than I did ten or fifteen years ago, largely because of all the monitoring activities that now take up our time! I still quite enjoy it though, and although not very artistic or creative, I take a pride in the symmetry and visual impact of the displays in my classroom.

I never throw out my coloured lettering from the display headings and have now amassed what I consider to be an impressive collection of letters in a variety of different colours and fonts, some of which have been used a number of times. Angling your stapler slightly as you affix the letters and the work onto the wall allows for easy removal and recycling of the letters and the backing paper (all work needs to be 'backed'; very occasionally I've even fallen victim to 'double backing' but that's almost unheard of these days as teachers are under such time pressures.) Sometimes, I've groaned inwardly when I've forgotten to pass on this tip to a Teaching Assistant or Parent Helper who is trying to be helpful with a display in my class. Staples inserted flat into the wall are much harder to remove and make recycling harder.

Linda and I do also spend some of our time monitoring planning folders. We ask to see them on a half-termly basis, and check that medium term plans are in place and properly evaluated at the end of a unit of work. Again, feedback on this may occasionally be given individually, but more commonly it is done in general terms through staff meetings. I do hear colleagues talk about heads in other schools who expect copies of detailed weekly planning on their desks every Monday morning, but none of the heads I have worked for have ever gone down this road, preferring to trust their teachers to get on with the teaching. Having spent some time as an Acting Head, I agree with this approach; I think you soon get to learn if a teacher is struggling and needs support through other avenues- you can then look to see if they need support with their planning.

My Shared Writing observation passes off successfully and Linda is pleased with what she sees. My class are enthusiastic and respond well to the activities. Whether all this monitoring will get the school a more positive judgement next time we have a full inspection, only time will tell.

Chapter 26

"If you fail to plan, you plan to fail."

Wednesday, 5th October 2011

This morning, as part of our ongoing programme of monitoring, my colleague Ruth is coming to watch me teach 4H maths. This means I have done something which is a rarity these days- I've written a lesson plan! It is standard practice, though, to prepare a lesson plan if you're being formally observed. Despite the famous quote above, attributed to the renowned scientist and politician Benjamin Franklin, most teachers do not, in my experience, write a detailed lesson plan for every lesson.

Certainly, I did for all my teaching practices whilst at college, and this continued into my probationary year at Lyndhurst, when Shirley checked my planning file periodically, just to check I was giving some thought to what I was doing. But the reality is that if you tried to continue this through your whole career, you would go mad. There are simply too many other things to be getting on with.

That is not to say teachers don't plan at all. Since 2005, it has been the right of all teachers to have a weekly, timetabled PPA session. PPA stands for Planning, Preparation and Assessment, and it should take up 10% (i.e. one morning or one afternoon) of the working week. So, every Thursday afternoon, I sit down in the Resources Room (a teachers' working space in between the Head's office and the staff room) with my current year group partner, Nicola, and plan the lessons for the next week. Previously, we had to do this in our own time either at lunchtimes or after school, so it is a welcome initiative. But we don't write individual lesson plans- there isn't time. We agree on the general content, maybe chat about approaches to take within the lesson and prepare the resources we're going to need.

Of course, this means that there needs to be somebody else in class whilst the teachers are having their PPA time (my class actually have a different face two afternoons a week, because I get a second afternoon out of the classroom to carry out my Deputy Head tasks.) Schools have tackled this problem in different ways; some have employed an extra part time teacher, some have taken on sports coaches to teach PE during PPA time and some have relied on Teaching Assistants to provide the cover.

We have taken the third of these options. Our cover is provided by our two excellent HLTAs, Hannah and Deanna. These two could easily both be teachers if they wanted to, and once or twice I've gently encouraged them to explore that possibility. HLTA stands for Higher Level Teaching Assistant, and this role was created in 2003 as part of the government's efforts to reduce teacher workload and raise standards in schools. To become a HLTA, you undertake some extra training and receive a bit more pay. It's not a lot and I worry about how sustainable this system is in the long term- if the Teaching Assistant workforce were to become unionised and the rates of pay become a political issue, I can see strikes aplenty. But maybe I'm being overly pessimistic; undoubtedly being a Teaching Assistant offers a potentially satisfying and rewarding job combined with the convenience of term time only work if you have school age children of your own.

Back to my lesson plan for this morning's maths lesson. What does it contain? We've had quite a bit of training on this recently from the two County Advisers currently working with the school, Julia for maths and Kathy for Literacy.

The first and arguably most important part is the learning objective. What are you hoping the children will be able to do by the end of the lesson? Teachers are encouraged to write the learning objectives for the day up on the whiteboard for the pupils to have in their minds throughout the lesson.

The next part of the plan is what's now called the 'starter'; how are you going to begin the lesson? In maths, it's usually a mental arithmetic task of some sort to get everybody's brain switched into maths mode, and today I'm going with an old favourite of mine, 'Fizz Buzz'- a game aimed at improving times tables knowledge.

Next, we move onto the main content of the lesson. Today's session is about column subtraction, so my plan explains that I will guide the whole class through a few examples on the board. Then, the children will be working independently for a while at subtraction questions of differing levels of complexity. The plan notes an example of each of these, resources that will be used to support those that find the concept tricky, and how my TA will be deployed.

Finally, the plenary involves some marking of the children's answers, an exploration of common errors and the children doing some self-assessment of how well they think they have understood the lesson.

It's important, of course, not to be a slave to your lesson plan, but to be flexible in your approach. If it turns out that a large part of the class do not have existing knowledge that you expected, you might have to 'think on your feet' and change tack- the same applies if they know a lot more than you thought. These scenarios are much more likely at the start of topics and/or early in the school year, when you are still getting to know the class.

Ruth conducts a very professional observation and spends a lot of time with the children at their desks asking them about their work. She is passionate about maths and improving our standards. I am reasonably content with how the lesson went but am sure I will be given some useful things to think about when I meet with Ruth tomorrow for the feedback.

Chapter 27

Can we just get on with the job now please?!

Tuesday, 16th October 2012

At tonight's Governors' meeting, there is an atmosphere of pride and relief. For the first time in several years, we are again sitting in a school that is officially considered "Good." And in some respects, an "Outstanding" one. The OFSTED inspectors called again in early July. In some ways, this is an awful time of year to get "the call"- with just three weeks or so of the school year left, the majority of teachers are running low on energy and emotional resilience. However, in other respects, it worked to our advantage. OFSTED do not generally like schools to change pre-planned events because of an inspection. So, the matinee production of the school play starring our Year Six pupils went ahead on one of the inspection afternoons, and even better from my point of view, on the morning of the second day of the inspection, Nicola and I left with the whole of Year Four for our annual three-day camping trip. All these activities going on also helped create for the inspectors a positive picture of the school- one pupil said to an inspector, "I bet you can't believe how exciting it is here," and that quote was the final sentence of the published report, which was a nice touch.

The inspectors acknowledged all the work that has been going on since the last inspection to try and improve our practices. High attainment, positive pupil attitudes, passionate school leadership and good teaching were all commented upon. We couldn't quite attain the gold standard 'Outstanding' judgement because of the progress issue, which the inspectors linked to the need to sharpen our marking practices and make the 'next steps' needed in their work clearer to the pupils. Despite some lingering resentment amongst some of the staff and governors around the 'value added' issue for junior schools, which at times I still feel myself, I think we can be happy with the result. I remember leaning against a tree at Cuffley Camp when I took a call from Linda informing me of the outcome. The reception wasn't great, but I heard the word 'Good', and a weight lifted from my shoulders.

But our encounters with inspectors weren't quite done just yet. Last month, we had our latest SIAS inspection. SIAS stands for Statutory Inspection of Anglican Schools. We must submit to these as well as OFSTED as we are a church school. These inspections happen around every four to five years and focus exclusively on the teaching of RE, collective worship and the impact of the school's Christian vision on its pupils.

Church schools have been around in this country for a very long time- indeed the church took on the role of trying to educate the country's children well before the government did. In the first half of the nineteenth century, many thousands of schools were set up by the Church of England's National Society. Bishop Wood School, although it wasn't called that then, started life in this way in 1842 (the three roomed building cost £800 to construct!) Of course, part of the reason for this was to instruct the children in Christian beliefs, but the 3Rs of reading, writing and arithmetic often featured on the fledgling curriculum too. It should be remembered as well that these schools were generally not set up for the benefit of the rich elite of society, but very often for the poor children of an area. Mind you, in the absence of state grants, teachers' salaries and the upkeep of the buildings had to be paid for somehow, and children attending the forerunner to Bishop Wood in the 1840s had to pay one old penny a week for the privilege. It was not until the Education Act of 1870 that the government started to exert its influence and schools without a specifically religious character, and completely free to the pupils, began to emerge. The 1944 Education Act re-established in law the current dual system of schools with and without a religious character. About 30% of schools in this country are now what are known as 'faith schools'- mainly Christian, but also Muslim, Sikh, Jewish, Hindu and so on.

Neither of the previous schools I worked in were faith schools, but I can't say the fact that Bishop Wood is has made a huge difference to my day to day working life. Although not a regular churchgoer myself, I have a personal faith of sorts and am certainly in sympathy with the Christian values that the school espouses. The school probably teaches a little more about Christianity in RE lessons than was the case at the other two schools, but we still teach the children about other major world religions too, and rightly so. Some of the assemblies are more overtly religious, and we make regular trips over the road to the parish church. Huw, the local vicar, is automatically a Governor, and a majority of Governors are 'Foundation Governors', effectively nominated by the church. Interestingly, as it is a Church School, the school gets to create its own admission policy, but this is based more on the location of the child's home than any other factors. Indeed, across Tring, parents largely send their children to the closest school. I doubt there are more than a handful who actively elect to send them to us because we are a church school, or who send them elsewhere because they are not.

Boosted by the positive OFSTED inspection in the summer, there was a positive feeling around the SIAS as soon as we got the call. We knew that, historically, many of the things that the inspection focuses on we have done well, and we knew that, from previous experience, there is a slightly different feel to these inspections than to OFSTED, with a sense that the inspector is looking for the things you're doing well rather than trying to find things that you're struggling with. In Linda and Harriet, our RE Co-ordinator, we had two passionate advocates of the school vision. We were given several weeks' notice of the inspection and prepared well beforehand in staff meetings and individually with our lesson planning. I had an enjoyable session with two Year Six pupils who were primed to give the inspector an early morning tour of the school, highlighting all the things that we wanted to emphasise as good examples of our work as a Church School. And it worked! On the day of the inspection, the school came together to show ourselves off at our best, and we were ultimately awarded an "Outstanding" SIAS judgement.

In this evening's Governors' meeting, as discussions around how we can continue to move the school forward inevitably continue, there is also a satisfied sense of a job well done. A feeling that, after a period of intense outside scrutiny, we will now hopefully be left alone for a while and just allowed to get on with the job. Mr Gove or one of his minions still hasn't seen fit to reply to the letter Huw and I sent about the 'value added' issue, but tonight, I don't really care!

Chapter 28

"We're quicker than the AA you know!"

Tuesday, 1st October 2013

Today is an ordinary working day. But it might not have been. Lots of schools across the East of England, and other regions, are closed or partially closed today due to industrial action by members of the National Union of Teachers (NUT.)

I have been a member of the NUT since student days, when we were offered free membership, which from memory even continued for my probationary year. The NUT is comfortably the largest of the teaching unions in this country, and it has the reputation of being the most left wing and militant. I do not consider myself an extremist in these matters but having studied the history of Trade Unionism and the struggles of the Tolpuddle Martyrs and the like, I am a believer in the right of workers to come together and defend their interests when necessary.

There is no compulsion in belonging to a teaching union just because you happen to be a teacher. I know of a few teachers who choose not to be, for reasons of politics, apathy or cost. My own view is that it is worthwhile belonging to one, if only for the legal advice and backing that they can offer. Back in my Fair Field days, a colleague and I got into some hot water over a decision to change a child's rooming arrangements on a school journey while we were away. On our return, the parents were very cross about this, and the school was forced to hold an enquiry into our actions. I contacted the union, and they had someone at the school about three quarters of an hour later to advise me as to my rights in this tricky situation. "We're quicker than the AA you know!", the cheery union rep had remarked when I complimented him on his speedy arrival. In the end, nothing major came of the enquiry, but I certainly appreciated having the backing of the NUT man that day.

Since early on in my time at Bishop Wood, I've been the NUT School Rep. The union likes to have a named point of contact in every school. It hasn't, to be honest, been too onerous a task. All the union post comes addressed to me, so I dutifully open it and keep the union noticeboard in the Resources Room suitably covered with information about the union's latest campaigns. The motions for conference booklet that comes out in the Spring Term usually makes for interesting reading and is a good way of keeping on top of what are the hot topics in education at any given moment, and what is happening around the world, as the union is very much international as well as national in its outlook. The NUT Annual Conference always takes place in the Easter holidays; I've never attended and am always impressed that some teachers are passionate enough about their work and wider causes to give up four days of their break to head off to Blackpool or wherever it is and discuss them.

Back at Bishop Wood, if a new member of staff joins the school, I always ask if they're in a union, and if they're not, I thrust an NUT application form into their hand. Occasionally, I might get asked for some advice with my union rep hat on; usually this will be to do with pay or perhaps workload. If I don't know the answer, I always point the teacher in the direction of the excellent Hertfordshire local reps, or the similarly helpful regional office, which for us, as we're in the East of England region, is based in Newmarket.

The decision to strike or not is never an easy one. Whilst articles in *The Daily Mail* and similar publications might suggest that lazy teachers are all too ready to take a day off, the reality in my experience is very different. For one thing, you lose a day's pay, and for some colleagues that makes already stretched household budgets even more difficult to manage. We do not underestimate the aggravation and inconvenience caused to parents if a school is closed on a day when it is supposed to be open. Some teachers hold the view that we should never strike under any circumstances, and indeed one union, PAT (Professional Association of Teachers), has this as one of their rules for its members.

It is the decision of the Headteacher to close or partially close the school, and teachers are under no legal obligation to inform the Head of their intention to strike before the day itself. A hardline union man (or woman) would probably exercise this right, but in the opinion of the majority of my colleagues and I, this is unnecessarily obstructive, so we try and give parents as much notice as possible of any strike action that we are going to take. Even if a strike is called by the union leadership, individual teachers do not have to support it. As we are a small school, and because virtually all our teachers are NUT members, if strike action is called, I will convene a meeting. We discuss the pros and cons of supporting the strike, and try to reach a consensus, which up to now we always have. It would probably cause a whole lot more problems if some teachers supported the strike and others didn't.

There have been occasions in the past when we have chosen to come out on strike. In 2002, we supported some action around the campaign to boost the London 'Fringe' allowance, a small annual top up to salaries for those of us employed on the edge of the capital. At the time, this amounted to just under £800 per annum, enough perhaps to pay my petrol money to work, but certainly woefully inadequate in terms of encouraging young teachers to apply for jobs in an area where rental costs were and still are massive. I was lucky when I first got a job with Hertfordshire- I was able to secure a 'teacher's flat' in Borehamwood at a very cheap monthly rental, but such luxuries have been hard to come by for many years now. At the time of that strike, I wrote to all the parents explaining our reasons for supporting it. I'm sure this wasn't universally welcomed, but at least we were trying to communicate our reasons for withdrawing our labour.

In 2008, we supported another NUT strike, again related to pay issues. With inflation running at just over 4%, teachers were offered a pay rise of less than 2 and a half %. This was again just a one-day strike in late April of that year, but it turned into quite a major event, with an estimated 8000 schools affected and some newspapers saying it was the biggest strike in the UK in terms of numbers participating for more than twenty years. As I wasn't in the classroom, I joined a union meeting and rally in Letchworth. I suggested in the meeting that parents might be more inclined to support future action if we confined it to boycotting SATs or similar, rather than completely refusing to work and forcing school closures.

Back in 2013, we are popular with the parents today as we've decided to work and not support the strike, which has been called due to concerns over pay, pensions and working conditions. This is not the 1980s miners' strike, so we didn't have to drive past any flying pickets to get into the school site this morning. I personally had voted to support the action, but only 27% of all NUT members across the country had bothered to vote, so I was happy to go with the majority of Bishop Wood teachers who decided it wasn't for them this time.

Although trades unions are not everybody's cup of tea, in my opinion, teaching unions are a good thing for teachers. They give us a sense of togetherness, and a feeling that someone has got our backs if things go wrong, or we make a mistake. I enjoy a flick through the quarterly magazines, and certainly don't begrudge paying my monthly subscription.

Chapter 29

The 'Curriculum Tsar' talks through his plans.

Wednesday, 8th October 2014

The Governors' Curriculum Committee has recently changed its name to the Teaching and Learning Committee. At the start of each academic year, the committees now review their 'terms of reference'- i.e. what they will be talking about and taking decisions on during their discussions. It was felt that the word 'curriculum' was rather a narrow title for the work of this group, hence the change. This evening, my job is to present to the committee the plans for the development of each subject during the coming academic year.

School Development Plans (SDP) have been around for years. At one point they changed their name to School Improvement Plans (SIP), but that seems to have gone out of fashion again, possibly because some advisers are now called School Improvement Partners, and there's potential confusion there. Anyhow, a School Development Plan does exactly what it says on the tin- it sets out how a school is hoping to change things for the better. Priorities and goals are set, and actions needed to achieve them are listed. Timescales, costs, personnel involved and how the success of the plan will be measured are all included too.

There has been some debate around at what time of the academic year a School Development Plan should be written. The worlds of education and business are not always easily intertwined, and here is a case in point. Although the academic year in the UK runs from September to July (with August off for re-charging of very flat batteries), the financial year runs from April to April, meaning school budgets are generally set in May once the amount of money devolved from central, and then local, government is known. It has been argued, because the finances are part of the plan, that SDPs should run from

April to April. This brings with it other problems, though- for example most staff changes happen in the summer. Generally, we have followed the model of creating ideas for the plan in the second half of the summer term once finances and personnel are known, publish the new plan in September, work on it for two terms and then review the impact before writing the next one in the summer again.

So, this year's plan is already known and tonight I will be talking the Governors through the subject specific aspects of that plan and answering any questions they have about it. As part of my Deputy Head job description, I have the overall responsibility for the curriculum at our school. For a while, I was even known amongst the staff as the 'Curriculum Tsar.' This is not to say they think I'm some sort of Russian despot; successive governments have appointed various people to be the tsar of this or that for some years now, and somehow my role adopted the term. My colleague Angela, a highly organised and competent teacher, who I remember for one of the best interview performances I have ever witnessed when she got the job here, is about the only member of staff who still refers to me as the 'Curriculum Tsar' as it amuses her, and I must admit it does have a certain ring to it!

Ruth is currently the Teacher Governor and at the meeting, so she talks first about her plans for Numeracy (maths) this year. Then I do the rest. Last month, a new version of the National Curriculum was introduced and some of our plans relate to the implementation of that. We're introducing a new spelling scheme in Literacy and trying to focus more on speaking and listening skills, which have arguably lost out to the more testable reading and writing.

Of the foundation subjects, the history curriculum is one of the most changed; there has been a move away from concentrating mainly on British history, and towards a bit more of a whole-world view, as well as a requirement to teach chronologically across a key stage (for example, don't teach World War Two before The Tudors.) Both these issues provoke an interesting discussion amongst the Governors. In music, there is also a somewhat altered curriculum to get to grips with, and we have purchased a new online resource to help us deliver it.

In PE, there are also big changes happening. Last year, partly as a way of ensuring a sporting legacy to our hosting of the 2012 Olympics, the government announced that schools would receive as part of their budget a sum of money (for us amounting to just over £10,000 per annum) known as the School Sports Premium. We have decided to spend our money on appointing a School Sports Apprentice to help deliver some curriculum and extra- curricular PE. Jack started work here last month and is already making quite an impression on the children, not least because he is wheelchair bound. He is such a great role model for the children, as they can see, just like we all did when the Paralympics were on, that people with a disability can do great things.

Sometimes, for older teachers like me (I turned 50 in the summer!) it is easy to feel cynical when another School Development Plan rolls around. Here we go again with another plan that has targets on that we may never have the time to implement. Certainly, some aspects of the plans can get lost in the hurly burly of a busy school year. But over the years, I think they've helped us achieve a lot and move things forward. How effective this year's version will be, we will have to wait and see.

Chapter 30

'Prevent' and British Values.

Wednesday, 14th October 2015

More training for me this afternoon, with my colleague Harriet. We are off to a posh local hotel for what is a half day's 'Wrap Training.' Wrap stands for 'Workshop to Raise Awareness of Prevent.'

'Prevent' has been around for over ten years now and has its origins in the horrific events of September 11th, 2001 in New York. '9/11' is one of those events that people can remember where they were when they heard the news. I can still see in my mind's eye a colleague of mine telling me about it in the school dining hall at the end of the school day. The '7/7'attacks in London four years later brought the issue closer to home. Since then, the government have been concerned with preventing 'home grown' terrorism.

Earlier this year, a decade on from the London atrocities, the government passed a Counter Terrorism and Security Act. As part of this, the 'Prevent Statutory Duty' was created, and this is now part of our wider safeguarding responsibilities. If you had told my 1986 self that one day I would be attending a course designed to spot the signs of children in my care becoming radicalised, I wouldn't have believed (or even understood) you, but here I am.

The 'Prevent' duty needs to be seen as part of another initiative in schools which is currently being pushed quite hard; 'British Values.' These values are democracy, the rule of law, respect/tolerance and individual liberty. It is now a statutory duty for schools to promote these values, and we are being told that OFSTED reports will comment on how well schools do this. Clearly, if you are trying to radicalise someone into potentially undertaking terrorist acts, you are in breach of all of these values, so schools and teachers are at liberty to intervene to try and 'Prevent' it. These values are being emphasised at our school through PSHE & C lessons (the 'C' stands for citizenship), history lessons (although there is a little less British history, the values still come up quite a bit), extra-curricular things such as School Council and, on occasions, in assemblies.

Harriet and I take our places in the meeting room along with lots of senior staff from other local schools. Linda will be going on a headteacher's course about this as well next week, and afterwards she, Harriet and I will be briefing the rest of the staff on what we've learnt and what our new responsibilities are.

The training, we are told on the opening slide of the PowerPoint presentation, has three main aims: to raise awareness amongst teachers about the risks of radicalisation, to help staff support those at risk, and to provide guidance on how to respond appropriately. It is also pointed out that other 'frontline' public sector workers such as the police, social services, probation and NHS staff are all receiving similar training as well.

The afternoon brings out a number of different feelings in me. Part of me thinks, "is this really part of a teacher's job?" I think back to all the extra tasks that have been foisted on us in the last thirty odd years. I worry too about the effects this could have on teachers' relationships with their pupils- what if a concern is raised and it turns out to be ill-founded? We are told that any intervention is only carried out with the agreement of the child's family, through a so-called 'Channel Panel', but is there still not a danger that such a process could damage the vitally important dynamic between family and school for years, and open the teacher up to allegations of racism, Islamophobia and goodness knows what?

On the other hand, particularly as an ex-Luton resident, I am haunted by that picture, shown regularly in the media, of those four young men caught on CCTV at Luton train station on the morning of the 7/7 attacks. Three of the four had been educated in the UK, and perhaps, if 'Prevent' or something similar had been around then, they and their 52 victims might still be alive today.

Hertfordshire is a diverse county. Whilst in some areas, such as Watford, there is a large Muslim population, our area is more monocultural. The training is being carried out on a regional basis and the facilitators explain that in our part of the county, it is more likely that people are in danger of being radicalised into joining 'far-right' racist groups rather than extreme Muslim ones. Those of us in primary schools are further advised that we may be more likely to see behaviour that causes concern in the parents rather than the children, but we should be on the lookout for this too.

My head is quite literally spinning as I head home. Tomorrow should be just an ordinary day with 4H, and after this afternoon, that'll suit me just fine.

Chapter 31

"Are you familiar with Instagram, Mr Hall?"

Monday, 3rd October 2016

If there is one sentence that makes a teacher's heart sink, it's one with the words 'bully', 'bullying' or 'bullied' in it. "That child is a bully." "There is a bullying problem in your school." "My son is being bullied." Quite often, those words will be followed up with something like "......and what are you going to do about it?" This always spells trouble; something nasty could be going on, and even if there isn't, it's going to take quite a bit of work to prove it. There are always a mixture of thoughts that run through your head at these moments. Concern for the alleged victim and their feelings of course. Who the characters involved are. What I might have to do in terms of investigating the bullying. What I might be able to do to stop it. Whether or not it's actually bullying.

I can't recall ever being bullied at primary school. I'm sure I would do if I had been, because one of the problems with school bullying, so research suggests, is that it can stay with you well into adult life and have a negative effect on you in many ways, including your mental health, job prospects and relationships. In the early days of secondary school, an older lad from another school extorted my bus fare change out of me two or three times on my walk home (this happened near a local sweet shop where at the time I think you could get ten 'black jack' or 'fruit salad' chews for 2p.) However, a quiet word from one of my mates at his school soon put a stop to that. I can remember being 'picked on' quite badly on two occasions at my own school, but these were short-lived agonies, and one of them was caused by me not being able to keep my mouth shut when verbally abused; having a go back led to physical punishment as well. Neither of these cases were really bullying.

Although I have never experienced bullying myself, it is my job this evening to lead the staff meeting about it. I begin by sharing with staff a definition of bullying. The government and charitable bodies agree that for bullying to be bullying it has to be repeated, intentional behaviour that involves an imbalance of power (i.e. the bully is older, bigger, stronger, more popular, etc than the victim.) The bullying may be physical or emotional. Often, but not always, the victim is targeted because they are a member of a particular group (racial, religious, etc.)

It has been a legal requirement for schools to have an Anti- Bullying Policy for many years now. The meeting moves on to look at our policy and remind staff of their responsibilities around implementing it. I remind my colleagues that the best way to deal with bullying is to prevent it happening in the first place, and there are lots of things we can do to make it less likely. The culture we create in school, the notion of us being a large extended family who look out for each other, is very important here. Allowing pupils to create their own Class Charters for behaviour at the start of each year, rewarding positive behaviour through our 'Golden Time' system and ensuring there are sufficient numbers of staff on duty at breaktimes and lunchtimes are all proactive actions that we take which hopefully feed into this positive culture.

However, bullying happens at times in every school, so what should our response be when it does occur? We teach about bullying in PSHE & C, usually having a particular focus on it around the time of Anti-Bullying Week in November of each year. The over-riding message behind these lessons is this: if you are being bullied, or know someone who is, doing nothing about it is not an option; that will only make things worse. You must tell a trusted adult, be it a parent, or a member of school staff about what is going on, so that they can begin to tackle the issue for you.

As the Deputy Head, issues around behaviour and bullying crop up as part of my job quite regularly. For a few years now, teachers have been keeping behaviour logs. Any transgression beyond the very minor is recorded briefly in these logs. I take the logs in and look at them as part of my Deputy Head time every half term. I analyse them in terms of the number and type of misdemeanour, look for trends and report periodically to the Governors Teaching and Learning Committee about my findings. I do encourage individual teachers to discuss with me at all times any issues they have within their class that they believe might be bullying; I like to have a whole-school view on the state of play on this at any given time. Often, there's no concerns, but sometimes there might be two or three that I'm aware of and working on.

When a new potential bullying issue comes to me, the first thing I must remind myself to do is to listen really carefully to the child (and his or her parents.) It is important that they feel the school is taking the issue seriously. I take notes and promise to do my best to resolve the issue. The next step is to speak to the alleged bully or bullies. Sometimes, they will immediately admit to the crime- usually, in this case I will say that if it stops straightaway and there is no repeat performance, they will hear nothing more about it. In this scenario, I consider myself lucky that not too much of my time has been taken up, but it is rarely this easy.

Quite often, the person accused of bullying will admit to it, but say the victim is also being unkind to them. An example of this happened a couple of years ago with a lad in my class. His parents came to see me saying that, at lunchtimes, he was being excluded from joining in with the class football matches and there was some name-calling and physicality involved too. This was in the Autumn Term and had been going on as far back as the previous academic year. When I questioned the two alleged ringleaders of the excluding, they admitted stopping him playing, but claimed that the reason for them doing so was that the boy was a 'bad loser' and started kicking out uncontrollably when his team were behind. After some tricky negotiations, it was agreed the boy would be allowed to play, and one of the Midday Supervisors undertook to keep an eye on the games and watch for any overly rough play.

If a child is feeling an outsider and excluded from play time and lunchtime activities, there are a couple of things that we can try. Nearly all our pupils are keen to help in this situation. I ask the person feeling left out who, in an ideal world, they would like to spend time with on the playground or the field; I encourage them, if they can, to come up with five or six names. I then get this group of children together and say something like, "X is having a tough time right now and is feeling left out at playtimes and lunchtimes. X has named you as people he/ she would like to play with. Would you be willing to commit to spend some time with him/her on a rota basis for the next few weeks?" It is rare for anyone to say no in this situation.

Such an approach is only sustainable, in my opinion, for a few weeks at most, and although it has helped solve some issues over the years, for more complex problems, something like the 'Circle of Friends' initiative can help. This is where weekly meetings take place of a group similar to the one described above, usually in lesson times and facilitated by a suitably trained Teaching Assistant. They undertake various activities with the aim of integrating more effectively into the group a child who is struggling to make and keep friends.

Back in the staff meeting, the discussion moves onto an aspect of bullying that has become more and more of an issue in recent years- online and cyberbullying. The continuing spread of the internet over ever-increasing aspects of our lives, and in particular the advent of smartphones, have both enriched and further complicated education in equal measure. Some of our older pupils now bring phones with them into school. Of course, a policy has had to be created to deal with this; we insist they are switched off and locked away during the school day. However, we cannot control what they do with them or other internet enabled devices once they are off the premises.

A year or so ago, on a day when I was in charge of the school, I was called to the Head's Office to be greeted by two police officers. "Are you familiar with Instagram, Mr Hall?" one of them asked. I had to confess my ignorance. It transpired that three or four of our Year 6 girls had been using this particular social media platform to trade some particularly unpleasant insults between each other. The police officers had printouts of these conversations, which they had been given by one of the parents. This was a difficult and, for us, very unusual case which necessitated several tricky meetings with the girls and their parents; in the end one of the girls actually left the school over it (out of choice- she wasn't excluded.) We now have a series of lessons in ICT (Information and Communication Technology) that teaches the children about online safety and in particular the many dangers involved in chatting online. These include not only befriending people you don't know and being careful not to divulge personal information, but also the fact that what you say in such chats is now there for all to see forever, as evidenced by the sheets the police officers showed me that morning.

Although we are a primary school, I finish the meeting by reminding my colleagues of our responsibilities around homophobic bullying. We have a part to play here to do with the use of language, and we have adopted a script, developed in another Hertfordshire school and recommended at training courses, to use when the word 'gay' is used as an insult. It very straightforwardly asks staff to remind children that 'gay' means a man who loves a man, or a woman who loves a woman, and that is OK, so 'gay' should not be used as an insult.

Dealing with bullying is not always one of my favourite parts of the job, but it can at times bring a sense of satisfaction and fulfilment when you play a small part in helping a child become more settled and happier in school. Hopefully, tonight's meeting has helped my colleagues feel more confident about the school's approach to this aspect of our work.

Chapter 32

"Are you sure she isn't your Mum?!"

Friday, 6th October 2017

This afternoon, I am meeting Natalie, the director of the company providing our new 'Wraparound Care' facility at Bishop Wood. Recently, it has become a requirement for all schools to offer this or provide a good reason why they're not (for example, you do not have enough space, there is no significant demand for it, or there are lots of other local options.) Wraparound Care is childcare that takes place before and after school on the school site and reflects the fact that in the majority of families nowadays, even in affluent areas like Tring, both parents are working and need help with their childcare outside of normal school hours. In our case, it is provided by Natalie's 'Breakfast and Supper Club' that operates in the school dining hall between 7.30am and 8.50am, and then again between 3.30pm and 6pm. Parents can choose to sign up for any or all of the ten weekly sessions, at a cost of course. A range of activities are provided, as are breakfast and a light snack in the afternoon. The club started earlier this year and has proved very popular with the parents and pupils.

The meeting is a regular monthly review of how the club is going, and the reason I am involved is that I am, for this term only, again the Acting Headteacher of the school. Linda left her post in the summer having been our Headteacher for thirteen years. We had another OFSTED inspection in January, and the outcome was that again we were rated 'Good.' The report praised the school in many, many ways and I felt a great sense of pride reading it through. However, Linda and I had been told in a meeting before the start of school on the day of the inspection that we could not be 'Outstanding' because the absence rates of our disadvantaged and SEN pupils were too high. When we subsequently investigated this, these figures were skewed by two children from a family who were going through an incredibly challenging period, but there was nothing we could do but take it on the chin and re-double our efforts to tighten up our procedures for monitoring attendance. It felt harsh; of all the balls we had successfully juggled, this was the one that we had dropped, and it prevented us receiving the ultimate accolade.

The lady inspector on this occasion happened to share my very common surname, and at the start of the day I had told 4H that a Mrs Hall would be popping in and out of some of our lessons, but that she was no relation to me. When she departed from one of her brief stays in the classroom, I was half horrified and half very amused to hear one of my pupils say, rather too loudly for comfort, "Are you sure she isn't your Mum?!"

Linda had been asked a few times in recent years to think about joining the County Advisory team. I think they were impressed, as we all were, by her calm and considered leadership, her devotion to school improvement and laser-like focus on the well-being of her pupils and indeed the staff. The January inspection, when I think we arguably missed an 'Outstanding' judgement on a technicality, perhaps made up her mind that it was time to move on and she accepted a post with effect from last month.

One of the last things she had to do as our Head was to deal with the controversy around a 'Refugee Day' we had planned in school. This was arranged as part of our commitment to 'British Values', particularly focussing on the tolerance and respect aspects of these. A speaker had been booked to talk to the children about why people might choose to seek refuge in the UK, and where they might be coming from. When we told the parents of our plans for this, one of their number objected to it on the grounds that we were being overtly political, and took to social media and the airwaves of a local radio station to let everyone know his views. Linda fashioned a great response; she contacted the parents again, asking if they wanted the day to go ahead and requesting email responses. The office received over a hundred messages- not one was against the idea, so we didn't alter our plans.

Fortunately, this time the process of finding a new Headteacher was a less drawn-out affair. Last term, several candidates came along to a selection day and the Governors involved told me afterwards that they felt that any of them could have done a good job. Eventually, after long discussions, a man named Gary was chosen as the successful candidate; he will be starting work here in January as the appointment came too late for him to meet the notice requirements in time for September. So, I'm in the hot seat again!

Linda, typically, did a lot of work with me last term to help prepare for being Acting Head again. With the assistance of the Governors, we appointed three Acting Assistant Headteachers just for this term. We divided up all my usual Deputy's duties between them; Ruth, Elaine and Paula have all got my back and are already proving a great support to me. Again, like last time, I also have the support of a brilliant Chair of Governors in Beth, and regular visits from a great local head, Rob, in a mentoring role. So, I've got a good team around me, which they say is one of the key attributes of being a successful leader.

I already knew Rob reasonably well, as last year he and I were both members of a party of Heads, Deputies and Advisers from the St Albans Diocese that visited Rome on a retreat that Linda had actively encouraged me to go on, and that the Governors supported financially. It was my first time in the 'Eternal City' and I had a wonderful time exploring it with some great colleagues.

I think because this time I know the role is only up until Christmas, I'm slightly more relaxed about it, but there is still an awful lot to do! In the first month of term, we have already, amongst other things, inducted a newly qualified teacher, finalised the School Development Plan, interviewed and appointed two new teaching assistants, agreed a changed Homework Policy, established a Grounds Development Committee, arranged some quotes for getting some new electronic gates at the front of the school, done some SIAMS preparation (the M is because the Methodists are now in on the act too), appointed two new Governors, secured a temporary part time placement for one of our pupils in the local behavioural support centre, and run a European Day of Languages. It's been very full on!

My meeting with Natalie reveals she is happy with the numbers her club is attracting and with the working space she has. I flag up the dates of a couple of upcoming school events that will mean she will need to relocate her club from the dining hall for two evenings. We talk about some behavioural difficulties some of her staff are experiencing, and about two children I would like to use some Pupil Premium money to fund free places for them at Breakfast Club with a view to improving their attendance. It's a positive end to the week and I head off home very tired but reasonably confident that the good ship Bishop Wood is steering itself successfully through the icefields of the education world.

Chapter 33

'Imposter Syndrome' makes a brief appearance.

Friday, 19th October 2018

Over the course of my career, I've heard of several schools where the arrival of a new headteacher leads to huge changes, in both how things are done and who is doing them, as a change at the top often leads to wholesale staff changes not long afterwards. In many cases, I'm sure this has been what's required, but sometimes I think it's just change for change's sake, and not necessarily for the good of the school or its pupils. I am pleased to report that Gary has not tried to implement loads of new ideas during his first ten months or so, although today he is trying one of them out on us; we are having an Open Morning when the parents are invited into school for the first hour and a half of the day to see the school 'in action.'

As Deputy Head and occasional Acting Head, I've had plenty to do with the parents over the years. It's vital that we communicate well with them and are open to hearing their feedback, both good and bad. Parents always get a say at the time of school inspections, and so the way we engage with them is especially important. Last November, when SIAMS came calling towards the end of my term as Acting Head, I was particularly grateful to a small group of parents who met with the inspector and talked about how we fostered the spiritual and moral development of their children.

That inspection was a tough moment for me. I had been told unofficially by the Herts RE Advisory team that it would be unlikely a school would be inspected whilst an Acting Head was in place, and had assumed this was correct as the term wore on and we hadn't heard anything. On the day we got the call, in late November, I confess some tears were shed, and I wasn't sure I could get through the stress of it.

I had become the RE co-ordinator the previous Easter when the excellent Harriet had moved abroad, but because of my Acting Head responsibilities, I hadn't done much RE wise since the summer. With all hands-on deck, we managed to secure a 'good' judgement, not quite maintaining our previous SIAMS 'outstanding' grade, but in the circumstances something I was more than willing to settle for.

As Deputy Head, I've sent out many Parent Questionnaires to try and understand their views on things and always tried to write back afterwards explaining what the school proposes to do in response to their comments. Of all the issues these have covered, homework is probably the most commonly recurring theme.

Homework is devilishly difficult to get right, particularly in a primary school, and we've changed our approach on several occasions, sometimes on the back of parental feedback. On the one hand, there are those who argue that children of this age should not have homework at all. Just let them enjoy their childhood, attend their clubs and activities in the evenings and at weekends, and leave the formal learning for the classroom. To be honest, I have more than a little sympathy for this school of thought, especially when large amounts of my time are taken up marking it!

However, the reason I feel, somewhat reluctantly, that primary school homework is a necessary evil is down to my own experience as a child. My primary school back in the Seventies didn't set homework, but when I reached secondary school, I was suddenly faced with three or four pieces a night to complete, and that was a huge struggle to begin with. Knowing that our pupils will also have to do homework once they reach senior school leaves me feeling that we're not really doing our job properly if we don't prepare them by setting at least some homework to get them used to the idea of doing part of their learning out of the classroom. Some parents at the other end of the spectrum feel we don't set enough homework, and so the school position falls somewhere in the middle between nothing and lots. We've always had a policy of not requiring work to be handed in the next day, to allow families to fit the work around other commitments.

The other issue is what to do about children who persistently don't hand homework in. Although these children are in the minority at Bishop Wood, it hardly seems fair to punish them too harshly as in reality it often means simply that they don't have the support that other pupils do at home. Officially, we reserve the right to keep children in at playtimes and lunchtimes to complete tasks, but I've tended instead to reward children who've handed in all their work across the term with a small prize, hoping (sometimes forlornly) that across the year, this will have a ripple effect amongst the class.

This morning, as I prepare the classroom for my 'Open Morning' lessons, I am feeling a little nervous. Although I've been observed by many different types of visitors during my career, I cannot remember a scenario quite like this before. Of course, there have been individual parent helpers who have watched me in action, and I'm sure reported back to their peers outside the school gates, but never a potentially large group of parents from my current class all at once. The fact I'm Deputy Head cranks up the pressure another notch. Am I really an 'exemplary classroom practitioner' as all the adverts for such posts now seem to require? 'Imposter Syndrome' kicks in briefly.

As the whistle blows at five to nine, I put my 'game face' on. There is a short period while I take the register and get the class settled with no parents present, and I use this time to lay it on thick about my expectations for the next hour and a half. Some of the children are clearly excited about the imminent arrival of their Mum and/ or Dad.

Although parents are at liberty to wander into any class, of course most aim for their own child's class straightaway, and stay there for the majority of the time. Many of them sit with their offspring and talk to them about the work as the lessons proceed. The first half hour is taken up with 'Guided Reading.' The class is divided into five ability groups for this; I sit with one group reading and discussing a particular text, whilst the other four get on with tasks independently, based on different texts. This part of the day is sometimes problematic as it relies on the four groups not with me getting on quietly and efficiently on their own- a tough ask for some Y4s. However, the parents seem to have a civilising effect in this regard, and the session passes off smoothly.

Next, we have an hour of maths. The 'changeover' at 9.30 is not as seamless as I would like, and I note a few concerned glances from the parents as books and seating positions are changed amidst too much noise and general faffing about. However, my introduction to the maths lesson goes well, and by 9.50 the children are all hard at work, and there are some great conversations going on with the parents (about half the class have at least one parent with them.) On days such as this, I do things by the book, and make sure I leave ten minutes at the end for a proper plenary to review what we've learnt today.

Despite my earlier nerves, I later concede to Gary that this is a very good innovation. Feedback, both written (Gary has given each parent a slip of paper to write their thoughts on) and verbal, is very positive. Parents are appreciative of the teachers' efforts and particularly welcome the chance to see modern maths teaching methods in action, as they feel they've changed a lot since they were at school. In one case of a child in my class, it's been a bit of an eye-opener for his Mum to see how challenging he found some of the maths, and she promises to do more with him at home to support him- another big plus from the day from my point of view.

Chapter 34

My knuckles are rapped, and 'Fingers' is framed.

Tuesday, 1st October 2019

During the first part of the school day today, our Site Manager and our Health and Safety Governor will be touring the school looking at how safe the school is. This is part of the work of the Governors' Resources Committee (a combination of the old Finance and Personnel Committees, and to be welcomed because it has reduced the number of annual Governors meetings from 24 to 18!)

Us teachers are often reminded that we always need to be on the lookout for potential 'H&S' hazards and report any concerns to the Site Manager. The term Site Manager has replaced Caretaker in many schools during recent years, as it more accurately reflects the wide range of jobs that the postholder gets involved in. Our current incumbent, Sally, is as likely to be on her computer sourcing quotes for work that needs doing round the school or liaising with cleaning companies as she is to be halfway up a ladder fixing a broken blind mechanism.

Health and Safety in its widest sense has become a much bigger part of everyday life as I've got older, and this has inevitably filtered down into the education world. Safeguarding is now a huge part of a school's work and has been for many years, with extra layers of responsibility gradually added, often in response to tragic deaths, in the hope that new rules will prevent a recurrence. One important change at Bishop Wood that Gary has insisted on since his arrival is the installation of electronic gates at the front of the school. This means that when the school is in session, visitors can only gain access having first spoken to the school office via intercom. Although this can be frustrating for bona fide visitors who arrive at the school when a member of the office team is not readily available, it is now more than 20 years since the Dunblane Massacre, and we have probably been guilty of naively assuming such a terrible thing couldn't possibly happen in sleepy Tring; Gary has now lessened the chances of it doing so.

When I first started teaching, I have a vague recollection of signing something to say I did not have any criminal convictions, and I suppose someone somewhere may have checked that I was telling the truth. Around the turn of the century, this was formalised with the establishment of the Criminal Records Bureau (CRB), and all teachers and other professionals wanting to work with children had to send their details to this body in order to have their credentials checked. This was replaced some years later by the Disclosure and Barring Service (DBS), who carry out checks and maintain lists of those not allowed to work with children. One of the first things an OFSTED inspector does these days is check that a school has up to date information on all its staff in this regard, and if any missing information is found, then the school can fail the inspection on these grounds alone.

These days, we even have a responsibility to keep our data safe. Last year there was a lot of chat (and some training) in school about GDPR (General Data Protection Regulation.) It's a European Union thing but apparently, even though we're leaving, the UK government is adopting it. We must keep any documentation about the children safely and securely stored (so our classroom cupboards now have digital locks on them) and obtain consent for using their photos in any number of different contexts. The school has appointed an external Data Protection Officer to advise us on all this, and he makes periodic visits to the school for updates with Gary and, on occasions, to lead staff meetings and keep us all informed on 'good practice' in this area. Christine, our Computing Co-ordinator, is the Deputy DPO and is responsible for logging any breaches of GDPR guidelines and potentially reporting serious ones to the Information Commissioner's Office. If someone leaves a vital piece of paper lying around (very easily done during a busy school day), or leaves their computer logged in and wanders off, we've had some fun shouting 'breach!' at the tops of our voices.

This may sound like we're trivialising our GDPR responsibilities, but I'm personally very cynical about such matters following an incident when I was Acting Head (for the second time.) The school had its knuckles rapped by the Information Commissioner because I had allegedly identified by name a parent to a Third Party (in this case a charity who were working with the school at the time.) I was innocent of this heinous crime. The charity already had this person's name as he had contacted them to ask them about the work they were proposing to do at our school. My offence had merely been to confirm it. The parent only made the complaint about me because he had an axe to grind against the school. By the time the official reprimand arrived from the ICO, Gary was in place as our new Head, and he persuaded me to try and forget about it, but I was hopping mad at the time.

Talking of things that drive me mad when it comes to Health and Safety, I should mention Evolve. This is a computer program that's been around for many years now and is used when planning any sort of school trip. It includes a requirement to conduct risk assessments for each visit, make sure staff are aware of potential hazards, and have appropriate safety measures in place. Now don't get me wrong; this is of course vital and any teacher would be daft to head off site with their children without having done their homework on such matters.

My problem with Evolve is two-fold. Firstly, each visit has to be uploaded and sent off to County for them to approve (and we get annoying e-mails after the trip reminding us that we haven't yet evaluated it.) As an experienced teacher, I absolutely hate the implication that I can't plan a trip properly and that I need some faceless bureaucrat to check my planning for me. Secondly, despite attending courses to try and get my head round how to use the program, I have singularly failed to do so and find it extremely frustrating. So much so that our long-suffering Office Manager Debs has in recent years, bless her, just done the blooming thing for me.

All this is not to say that I haven't enjoyed the many school trips and journeys I've been on over the years. 'Journeys' (i.e. residential overnight stays) have been amongst the most memorable parts of the job.

With younger juniors, I have visited Cuffley Camp on a number of occasions. This is within Hertfordshire and has the added benefit of proximity to home if any of the children really struggle with homesickness and need collecting early. This is also true of Buckinghamshire's Woodrow High House that we've used for our Year 4 journey for the last couple of years.

The Cuffley trips have been for just two or three nights and are usually pretty character building! They often become an exercise in conquering sleep deprivation. Years ago, all accommodation was in tents but more recently the staff have graduated to garden sheds with a bed inside. The trip usually happens at the height of summer but one year we went quite early in the term and our first night there was the coldest May night for fifteen years, with temperatures as low as -2 degrees Celsius; very little sleep was on offer that night. It's an activity holiday and the vast majority of children love taking part in shelter building, the assault course, campfire singsongs and the like.

Trips for Y6 pupils have been further afield to either the Isle of Wight or Norfolk, two parts of the country that I've come to really like as a result of my accompanying school trips there. These are slightly longer affairs lasting from Monday to Friday and are generally great fun. They nearly always happen in the last half term of the children's time at the school and the hope is that they will help to give them a memorable farewell to their primary education.

One year, when we had a particularly troublesome Year 6, we changed it up a bit and went in the Autumn Term in an attempt to build relationships and help the year group 'gel' together a bit better. It wasn't a resounding success; it got dark too early in the evenings, and we found it harder to keep the children occupied after the sun had gone down. This was also the time when one lad decided to barricade himself into his first-floor bedroom and threaten to jump out of the window. Fortunately, we somehow managed to break into his room before he did so. At that point, I made a phone call home and said to his mum either she comes and collects him now, or she comes and stays with us for the rest of the week and takes full responsibility for him. She chose the latter.

In the Isle of Wight, we tended to stay at the PGL adventure holiday site at Whitecliff Bay near Bembridge. The staff liked to tell our pupils that PGL stands for 'Parents Get Lost', but in fact it stands for Peter Gordon Lawrence, the founder of the company. There we took part in activities such as water sports, abseiling and fencing, and visited local sites such as Osborne House (Queen Victoria's country retreat), Black Gang Chine and The Needles. Both my daughters tagged along in their pre-school days, and it was interesting to note that some of the livelier boys in the class were invariably at the front of the queue when it came to pushchair duties!

In Norfolk, we stayed at a lovely large hotel overlooking the sea at Overstrand near Cromer. The highlight of this week was always the day when we went on a boat trip seal watching, and then a long walk around the beautiful Blakeney Point area. At one point on that walk, you are three miles from the nearest road, and the instructors used to ask us all to lie down in the sand dunes, close our eyes and just listen to the sounds of nature around us. One year, the only sound we could hear was the rather loud snoring of Jason, one of our parent helpers. A few parents always came on these trips as extra pairs of hands, and they generally added to the fun. Once, some of them and I stayed out having a drink or two in the grounds of the hotel rather too late. We were locked out and I had to throw gravel at my colleague Liz's window to get her to come and let us in. I should mention here that we had a strict policy of one teacher always abstaining from alcohol every evening in case of emergencies; on at least one occasion, I can remember a late-night hospital visit with an injured pupil when it was my turn not to drink.

One year, our brilliant Teaching Assistant Hannah was the victim of a practical joke in Norfolk. She and her colleague Deanna had been in trouble with the rather officious hotel owner earlier in the week for moving a lamp. This really amused one of the dads who was with us, Nigel, and with my help we 'framed' Hannah as a petty thief. Nigel sourced a similar lamp from a local charity shop, we planted it in Hannah's bag and then I theatrically announced to the children as we were leaving Cromer on the Friday that the hotel owner had contacted me and said a lamp had gone missing and everybody's bag needed checking. When the lamp was found in Hannah's bag, I quickly made it clear to the children that it was a joke, but Hannah has had to put up with the nickname 'Fingers' ever since, and has her middle initial recorded as 'F' (even though it isn't) on the aforementioned Evolve. It's just as well she has a sense of humour.

Back in the present day, Sally and Edmund (the Governor) don't spend too long in my room on their tour of the school. They note a particularly leaky window, the cramped and potentially dangerous cloakroom that can so easily become a trip hazard when the coats fall off their pegs, and the rather tatty state of the ceiling. This and their other findings will now be reported back to the next Resources Committee meeting, where a plan of works to address the issues will be agreed upon.

Chapter 35

Dr Crippen makes it onto Twitter.

Wednesday, 21st October 2020

This morning the Senior Leadership team are meeting, as we always do on a Wednesday morning. Our agenda is somewhat different than it would have been just eight months or so ago and is dominated by our ongoing battle to deal with the Covid 19 pandemic. We are concerned this morning with managing an outbreak of cases in Year 4, (that's my year group, though mercifully I have managed to avoid catching Covid so far) and discussing the logistics of introducing 'Google Classroom' as a way of setting work for children at home who are self-isolating. It could also come in very handy if there are any further lockdowns, although I inwardly cringe when realising what a steep learning curve for technophobes like me it would be!

Recent events have been by far the most difficult for schools to deal with of my entire career. Like the rest of the country, I suppose the Covid 19 crisis crept up on us at school. From late January/ early February time, there was some chat in the staffroom about it, and I remember Gary led an assembly about the virus, and sensible precautions we could take in school. After half term, events involving large numbers of people began to be cancelled, and then, in the middle of March, we were told one Wednesday that the school would be closing at the end of the week and would only reopen the following Monday to vulnerable children and to children of 'key workers.' By now, there were real concerns amongst the staff for their own safety given the spread of this hitherto unknown illness. So, at extremely short notice, Gary had to organise two things very quickly. Firstly, a list of pupils who were eligible to still attend school. Secondly, a rota of teachers and teaching assistants who felt they were at sufficiently low risk of catching the virus or becoming seriously unwell with it that they were willing to help run the in-school sessions.

As Deputy Head, I really wanted to be part of this and help lead the school's response to the crisis. I considered myself fairly fit and healthy for a 55-year-old, but I suffer from asthma, and this made me potentially vulnerable, so after a fair bit of agonising, I decided discretion was the better part of valour, and informed Gary that I did not wish to be included in the rota. It was a most peculiar feeling walking out of the school that Friday evening, not knowing when I would return. A couple of the parents, remarkably, had even sent in thank you/ end of year presents and cards, assuming we wouldn't be teaching their children again.

The Government issued guidance on who exactly was a 'key worker'; these included those working in health and social care, education, the justice system, the food industry, the armed and emergency services, transport and utilities. They also clarified what they meant by 'vulnerable' pupils- these were small in number for us, but included those with an Education and Health Care plan (the successor to 'Statements'), those with 'Child in Need' or Child Protection plans, 'Looked After' children and adopted children. Most of our parents took the 'key workers' list at face value, and did not attempt to have their children included in the on-site lessons unless they really did work in the specified industries. There were a few who tried it on though, including one lady who tried to argue that her job at a horse stable should qualify her son to attend. In the end, numbers of pupils who continued to come to school varied between about 10 and 15% of the total on roll.

We had two weeks between the closure of the school and the Easter holidays. During that period, and then again for another five weeks between Easter and the Whitsun half term, those of us not teaching in school were working from home, setting work and giving feedback on completed assignments via email. I was impressed with the amount of work that was done given the fact that parents would have been juggling their supervision of the tasks we set with their own work responsibilities.

It must have been really tough for them; I constantly found myself feeling grateful that both my children were well beyond school age and fending for themselves. A friend of mine with four school age children sent me a message towards the end of the first week of the lockdown asking me how the hell I did what I did for a living, and saying he'd suspended two of his children already! Perfectly understandably, more priority was given to the Maths and English tasks that we set in the morning, compared to the other subjects that were set in the afternoons. On a typical day, I would say about 80% of the class would do the Maths and English, with that dropping to perhaps 50% for the rest. The few who produced little or no work were contacted by email (or by phone by the SENCO) and offered support to try and up their output. One of our teachers delivered weekly printed work packs by hand to those who didn't have access to reliable internet or a PC, and in some cases we were able to send home a PC for their use.

As well as the work via email, we tried to stay in touch with our classes by producing weekly videos that were uploaded onto 'You Tube' for them to view. Once I conquered the inevitable technical challenges, I came to quite enjoy these. The one I particularly remember is when I laid out my ties on the sofa (I was amazed to discover I had 44 of them!) and asked the class to design a new one for me as an Art exercise. Quite a few had a go, and the winning design was expertly turned into a real tie for me by our very creative Site Manager, Sally, so I now have 45 ties! I also recorded a whole school worship or two from my kitchen table, and with the help of Chris, our resourceful Computing co-ordinator, all the staff contributed to a video featuring us all drinking tea to the tune of 'You got a Friend in me.'

It was a strange, strange time. Living on my own, I was especially grateful for the beautiful weather and the chance to explore the countryside around Tring (I moved here last year), even if it was difficult to maintain the required 'social distancing' rules and stay two metres apart when passing fellow walkers on the nearby canal towpath.

As the weeks drifted past, there were murmurings about Year Six returning to school on a part time basis after half term, in order to give them some sort of 'normal' ending to the primary phase of their education. I sat in on some NEU 'Zoom' briefings about this (the NEU is the National Education Union, formed a few years ago when the National Union of Teachers and the Association of Teachers and Lecturers merged.) Then, the week before half term, I returned to the school for the first time in around two months and met with Gary, Debs (our Office Manager) and Sally (our Site Manager) to discuss the practicalities of this from a Bishop Wood point of view. Debs is now something of an expert on the ever-changing Covid governmental advice and has spent many hours on the phone to the helpline seeking clarification on the latest proclamations.

A couple of days after this meeting, a whole staff gathering was held on the school field in which Gary went through our plans and asked us to consider our feelings about coming back to teach the returning Year Six pupils. Although one or two colleagues who were clinically very vulnerable still understandably thought this was too risky, most of us were now very keen to get back into school.

The two Year Six classes were split in half. Half of each class would be attending on Mondays and Tuesdays, and the other half on Wednesdays and Thursdays; this was to allow social distancing in the classrooms. The 'Key Workers'/ Vulnerable Pupils group was still operating every day, as was the programme of online learning for the other year groups. Myself and Carol, one of our brilliant team of Teaching Assistants, were assigned one of the Year Six groups, and it was great to be back doing 'proper teaching' again.

The experience of teaching in what has become known as 'The New Normal' was, however, quite different. Various precautions were taken to stop the potential spread of the virus. The school was festooned with black and yellow 'crime scene' type tape to help facilitate one-way systems and socially distanced queuing for your lunch. Desks were moved around so that each child had their own table; group work was a definite no-no! Each child had their own set of writing and drawing implements inside a named plastic wallet- they were not allowed to share items on pain of death! The advice was to 'quarantine' books for 72 hours before doing any marking, and even then, some of us wore protective plastic gloves when doing so- Gary snapped me so attired for a memorable photo placed on the school Twitter feed. Comments that I looked like Dr Crippen were a bit uncalled for, I thought.

All children had their temperature taken on entry to the classroom and any with a reading too high were escorted to the office and a phone call home made with a firm request to collect them as soon as possible. All hands had to be cleaned with gel on entry too. We were allowed to exercise our own judgement in terms of mask usage. Most of us opted for the clear plastic visor style. I tended to be maskless when teaching at the front of the class, but to don the visor when offering individual assistance at a child's desk. Fortunately, it being the summer, classroom doors and windows could be comfortably left open, so ventilation was not a problem. The teaching wasn't always easy. Although many of the children relished being back in school, this wasn't universally true. Some had got used to being at home and weren't really that interested in being there or the lessons being taught to them.

Although it wasn't statutorily required, we were keen to get the other year groups back into school before the end of the Summer Term if possible. This we managed, again in half groups, for a couple of days a week for the last few weeks of term, so I got to say a proper goodbye to 4H after all.

This term, the school is now of course operating with all pupils in every day. But there are quite a few differences to the situation pre-March. Year groups are in their own 'bubbles' and not allowed to mix-so playtimes and lunchtimes are staggered, and whole school events including assemblies aren't happening, although Huw and his superb curate Sarah are continuing with their weekly 'Zoom' assemblies, which are not only very thought provoking, but also extremely entertaining. Temperature checks and compulsory hand gelling on entry are continuing. Adults not employed by the school are not encouraged on the site, so any liaison with parents has to be done by phone or email rather than in person and plans to conduct next month's Parent Consultations by 'Zoom' or some similar wizardry are already well underway.

There is one silver lining to all this. In order to reduce the risk of spreading the virus, and to help observe social distancing guidelines, we have, like a lot of schools, allowed the children to come into school dressed in their PE kit on days when we are teaching them PE. I am already pretty sure that this is an innovation that will outlive the pandemic. The joy I feel when I realise that I will never again hear the dreaded words, "Mr Hall, I've forgotten my PE kit!" is hard to describe.

Chapter 36

"What is pornography, and would you recommend it?!"

Thursday, 21st October 2021

Life at school is now pretty much back to normal. However, we are still required to test ourselves for Covid twice a week and formally report the result to the school via email. Some of our staff have now had the virus, mercifully none seriously, but so far, I have still avoided it. The 'wear your PE kit to school on PE days' initiative is, as predicted, here to stay. Another change brought on by the Covid period but now likely to remain for the foreseeable future is the so called 'soft start' to the day. Instead of the children all congregating together on the playground and then lining up when the whistle goes at 8.55am, before trooping into school for registration, classrooms are now open for the children from 8.35am, although the register is still not taken until 8.55. This has added to the time teachers are required to be physically in the classroom and led to an earlier break up of pre-school gossiping in the staffroom, but has ensured a more ordered and less chaotic start to the school day.

Each classroom now has a carbon dioxide monitor fitted on the wall. I try and keep an eye on it but inevitably forget to once immersed in a lesson, so a nearby child is usually tasked with letting me know if the reading goes above 800 parts per million. This is the magic number that we have been advised to keep an eye out for, and I throw open windows and the classroom door once the number is exceeded; this usually has the desired effect, and the reading drops quite quickly.

I reflect again on the massive changes that I've seen during my career. Fifteen or twenty years ago, I occasionally employed a child to keep an eye on the Test Match score on a classroom computer. "Keep an eye on the number after the dash" (meaning the number of wickets down) I would say to a child sat near to one of the few computers connected to the internet, "if it changes, let me know!" At the end of one particularly fraught afternoon, I remember getting cross with a child who was raising his hand forlornly at the back of the room while I was trying to get the classroom tidy and the children ready for their dismissal. "What is it now, Iain?" I thundered. "Sorry, Mr Hall, that number has just changed." Cue an embarrassing climbdown by yours truly. If you'd told me then that years later the child in the corner of the room would be monitoring CO_2 levels rather than the cricket scores, I would have laughed at you.

The second lockdown at the start of this year was certainly more difficult than the first one, mainly I think because of the time of year. Speculation was increasing throughout the Christmas and New Year holiday that schools would have to close again because of the upsurge in Covid cases. The teaching unions were insisting it would be dangerous for schools to reopen as normal, but the Government was insisting that we should. Once again, I found myself involved in a series of Zoom and WhatsApp calls with the NEU and my colleagues about the situation. Then at the eleventh hour, the Government bowed to the inevitable and made the decision to close schools to most pupils again.

January to March was a grim time to be working from home. Cold and dark conditions meant the beautiful springtime walks of the previous lockdown were but a distant memory. Still, changes to how we delivered our remote learning kept me on my toes. This time, all tasks were set on 'Google Classroom' and we had regular 'Google Meets' with our classes. Google Classroom is a program that allows us to set tasks, the children to do them, message us with any queries, and us to 'mark' the work and provide feedback. To my surprise, after about a fortnight, I'd mastered this and felt reasonably confident that most of the class were accessing the learning as well as could be expected given the circumstances.

'Google Meets' were held a couple of times a week at first, but then more regularly as the lockdown wore on. These offered me the chance to speak to the whole class at once (at least in theory, although not all the children for various understandable reasons were always able to join.) I used these as an opportunity to offer guidance on the work, answer any questions, and sometimes hold a quiz. After a while, the children took them over somewhat and did their own presentations to the class on a subject of their choice.

These have carried on since we've been back in school. The old 'Golden Time' slot on a Friday afternoon, already somewhat outdated because it didn't really fit with new ideas around behaviour, was dealt a fatal blow by the year group 'bubbles' and the fact that children in different parts of the school were not allowed to mix. So, this time is now devoted to so-called 'Little Teacher' sessions, when the children, either individually or in pairs or small groups, present to the class about an interest or hobby. Current 4H look forward eagerly to these sessions and are keen to lead them.

This time, most of the staff, including myself, were happy to take our turn helping with the Key Worker/ Vulnerable Pupils group that was operating in school. This allowed us to have four separate groups, one for each year. My year group partner and I took it in turns and did 'one week on, one week off' teaching the Year 4 group, which usually contained between five and ten pupils, depending on the work commitments of the parents. The week before February half term was one of my weeks in school, and it was bitterly cold. By now, it was becoming clearer that Covid was an airborne virus, so quarantining books and Dr Crippen impressions weren't required, but ventilation most certainly was, so all the windows and the classroom door remained open most of the time. I taught that week in five layers and a bobble hat. One of the mothers of a child in our year group wrote a scathing email to Gary, which it was difficult not to sympathise with. "My child is unlikely to catch Covid", she wrote, "but could well die of hypothermia!" The guidance was clear though, and our hands were tied. It's been interesting to note that with windows open in much colder conditions than would have been the case before Covid, the number of children with coughs has reduced significantly.

I do think we (and no doubt other schools too) will have to work hard in the coming months to re-connect with parents. With them not encouraged onto the school site for so long, and with all communication confined to the phone or email, something has been lost. The power of the quick five- or ten-minute chat at the classroom door at the end of the day is not to be underestimated. Inevitably, people cannot always express themselves as clearly by email, and misunderstandings and irritations can develop, on both sides.

I wonder too about the long-term effects of the lockdowns on the work habits and attitudes of some of the children. If their parents were busy and were forced to give the children the option of not doing some of the online assignments, it is hardly surprising that now they're back in school, a minority of pupils are less than enthusiastic about completing some of the tasks we set them. They can get frustrated and fractious in a way that perhaps they wouldn't have done prior to the Covid period.

It would be daft to not address this issue and just to carry on as if Covid had never happened, so we have adapted some of our PSHE (Personal, Social and Health Education) lessons to try and do so. Personally, although it hasn't always been a statutory part of the curriculum, I have generally enjoyed teaching these lessons, as they address important issues and often lead to some excellent discussions with the children. My lesson with 4H this afternoon is one of those which tries to address the heightened emotions that the last eighteen months or so have led to in some pupils; we will be working on the 'Zones of Regulation.' This is one of a clever series of lessons which gets children talking and thinking about their feelings, and places those feelings into one of four 'zones.' These zones are given colours- blue, green, yellow and red. The ideal zone to be in is green and this is for feelings such as happy, calm, proud and focussed. However, you might be in the blue (sad, bored, tired or sick), yellow (worried, frustrated, silly or excited) or red (overjoyed, panicked, terrified or angry) zones instead. The lessons try to get children to recognise what zone they're in, and explore strategies for moving into the green zone, where you will learn more effectively, if you're not already there. It's interesting stuff and is bearing a little fruit already in 4H I would say.

One area of PSHE that has been constantly changing and has caused a lot of discussion during my time as a teacher has been Sex Education (often now referred to as SRE- Sex and Relationships Education.) I've taught this to my class most years, and sometimes, as one of the few male teachers in a primary school, I've been asked to teach it in other year groups if any of the lessons have been boys only (we've sometimes gone down this route because it has been felt pupils are more likely to discuss things more openly and ask more questions if there are only members of their gender in the room.)

The biggest change has undoubtedly been around LGBTQ+ issues. When I started teaching, there was something called 'Section' or 'Clause' 28, which forbade teachers from openly discussing homosexuality. The wise thing at the time was to not mention the subject at all. Happily, things are very different now, and we now teach that there are lots of different relationship and family types, all equally valid.

Parents have always had the right to withdraw their children from Sex Education lessons if they wish to, and over the years, a small number of parents in the schools that I've worked at have chosen to exercise that right. We've often invited parents into school beforehand to watch any videos we might be using, or in more recent years sent home online links for them to view. This has tended to allay any fears and minimise the number of children withdrawn.

There have been some memorable lessons over the years, and SRE does test your ability to think on your feet like no other lesson. If a child asks a question and you're fairly confident that they've asked it because they're genuinely curious and they're not just trying to shock you or impress their friends, then it probably deserves an answer. However, not all the children in the class might be quite ready to hear the answer, so sometimes an element of caution and a "you might like to ask your Mum or Dad about that one" or "you'll find out more about that at secondary school" type of answer may be the way to go.

In my second year of teaching, somehow we had got onto circumcision and foreskins, and a girl in my class, I think quite innocently, asked me if I had a foreskin. I employed mock outrage tactics and said that although I was happy for an open and frank discussion, I was not going to answer questions of such a personal nature! Many years later, at Bishop Wood, I was leading a lesson with Year Five boys on the subject of wet dreams. I think it was quite warm in the classroom (SRE tends to be left towards the end of the school year when you know your classes well), but this group found the subject or my presentation of it quite difficult to cope with; two boys fainted and a third also had to seek sanctuary in the medical room looking a very funny colour indeed. Probably my favourite question I've ever been asked in SRE came from a Year Six boy a couple of years ago, and this one was asked partly for shock value, I think. He asked, in a very 'well spoken' voice, "what is pornography and would you recommend it?" Once the inevitable tittering had died down, I was quite pleased with my reply which was something like, "by the look on your face, I think you know the answer to the first part of that question. As for part two, I'll buy you a pint in The Black Horse in ten years' time and we can discuss that." He and his smiling mates seemed to accept that.

Chapter 37

A funeral and a farewell.

Friday, 7th October 2022

Today is a sad and poignant day. This morning, I am attending the funeral of Pat, who was the school secretary at Bishop Wood for the first eight years or so of my time here. Gary is perfectly comfortable with me being out of school for the morning and willingly sanctions a supply teacher covering my class. In my experience, when an important figure at a school passes away, Headteachers are always keen to have a representative of the school present at the funeral, and rightly so in my opinion. There are lots of old colleagues present including my old boss, Brian, with whom I am able to have a long chat. The funeral is a fitting send off for a lovely lady and a truly brilliant school secretary who Brian described at her retirement do as "the single most important person at Bishop Wood."

I don't attend the wake, but instead head back to school for afternoon lessons. The school as always is marking Black History Month and I lead a lesson about the poetry of Benjamin Zephaniah, which provokes some interesting discussion in 4H. The school serves a largely white catchment area, which makes this sort of work even more important for us, and we have been working recently with a county adviser on tweaking our curriculum to ensure it is anti-racist.

A year or so ago I had a very interesting chat with one of our Governors, who happened to be black. He talked persuasively about the 'unconscious bias' that he felt many white teachers display towards ethnic minority pupils, and how the latter aren't always stretched academically in the same way that their white counterparts are. He stressed the importance of emphasising to the children the multicultural nature of the UK today and choosing British role models to focus on in school, rather than the usual international ones. His daughter, he said, had sat in too many lessons about the likes of Martin Luther King and Rosa Parks. Some very interesting food for thought for us.

Later in the day, I attend an afterschool 'pub club' to say farewell to one of our teaching assistants, Liz, who is moving onto a new school where she has been given more hours and more wide-ranging responsibilities. Gary was keen to set up after school trips to the pub on a Friday when he arrived, and these have started up again on a reasonably regular basis post-Covid. They're good for team building and a pleasant way to end the working week. I have known Liz for many years as both a colleague and a parent helper and she has been a great asset to the school and will be very much missed. It's a different type of send-off to the one I attended earlier in the day but still tinged with sadness.

These two events together put me in a reflective mood. I experience a growing realisation that I am now very much in the autumn of my career, if not heading into the winter! Glancing at my diary for next week, I remind myself that I have a Financial Planning webinar booked in for one evening, with a view to doing some sums about possible retirement. I still enjoy the job most of the time, and hardly ever wake up and don't want to go into school, but the physical and mental demands of the role are beginning to take their toll. I am very keen to go out at a time of my choosing, not when incompetence or ill-health forces me out.

It is harder these days for me to cope with the ever-increasing number of computer programs you need to master in this job. In the last couple of years, all scrapes, bumps and bangs on the head need to be recorded on something called Medical Tracker. I preferred the old book with strips of carbon paper in it so you could tear off a copy for the parents! Even more crucial to the job is a program on which we write and review our individual plans for SEND children in our classes. I'm really struggling to use this, and am regularly bailed out by our brilliant SENCO, Jane.

I find myself thinking about the example of Arsene Wenger a lot lately. Wenger was, by common consent, probably the greatest manager of Arsenal FC in the 135 years or so of their history. The longest serving man to hold the post, he was a highly intelligent visionary and a terrific man-manager. But he stayed on a bit too long and in the end was forced out because the team's results weren't good enough. I have now been at Bishop Wood longer than he was at Arsenal, and I don't want to suffer a similar fate.

Chapter 38

"Good but declining - and that's just the Deputy Head!"

Monday, 16th October 2023

Today is a fun day as we have one of our most regular and popular visitors in school- the 'Electric Umbrella' musical group. Founded by one of the dads from our school, it is a charity that gives adults with learning disabilities the chance to perform on stage. Our pupils love their visits and they're always great fun.

Today will probably be the last chance I get to see them, in this context at least, because I formally tendered my resignation on September 1st, and will be retiring next summer. It is both scary and exciting in equal measure, but as by next year I will have reached my 60th birthday and also completed twenty-five years in the school, it feels the time is right to go.

One of the moments that helped me to make my mind up came last February when we had a 'Safeguarding Check' carried out by one of the senior advisers from county. The visit went well and was in general a big vote of confidence for the school. But one technicality that we were picked up on really riled me and made me think that it was probably time for me to depart the stage of the education world.

One of our Year Five boys was at the time spending two or three afternoons a week at the local Behavioural Support unit. Despite the fact that this institution was in our own authority, apparently, we were still responsible for getting written confirmation from them that all of their staff had the appropriate DBS clearance. When I queried this, the lady carrying out the review, a highly respected figure, propped her folder up onto her knees, tapped it like it was some sort of sacred book and said, "well it says it in the guidelines!" With Gary's eyes piercing into my back and me inwardly acknowledging that now was not the time to rock the boat, I resisted the temptation to say, "I expect the Third Reich had guidelines- it doesn't mean they were all right or shouldn't have been questioned!" On reflection, no doubt this requirement must've come from somewhere, perhaps as a result of some terrible event in another part of the country when such confirmation had not been sought, but at the time it struck me as ridiculous and made me feel I belonged to a bygone era.

Shortly after this, we received the OFSTED call in March, the same week that the news of the tragic suicide of Headteacher Ruth Perry was all over the press. Even allowing for the extended break from inspections during the pandemic, this was only a little over six years since our last one, and in weak moments, I'd allowed myself to believe that maybe I had finished my encounters with OFSTED.

Nevertheless, Gary and I had done some preparation the previous summer knowing that it was a possibility, and we threw ourselves as positively as we could into the lengthy pre-inspection phone call the day before. This was a so-called 'ungraded' inspection and took place over two days with just one inspector. 'Ungraded' in the sense that it was a visit to check that we were still 'Good' like last time, but that the inspector did not actually have the power to officially reclassify us upwards or downwards if she suspected we weren't.

After the usual extremely draining forty-eight hours, the feedback was mixed. There were many strengths identified: the welcoming and friendly atmosphere, the happy and confident pupils, the broad curriculum, the quality of the extra-curricular provision and the visits programme, safeguarding, reading and SEND. However, concerns were raised over the clarity of the curriculum in some subjects (one of mine, Geography, was subject to a 'deep dive' and found wanting in this regard), together with how effectively children's understanding was checked before teachers moved on to the next part of a topic. The other issue was behaviour; it was felt staff expectations were not consistent across the school, and in some classes too much learning time was lost because pupils were distracted. This view was supported by some of the parental feedback given in the online questionnaire.

All this led to the disappointing outcome that the inspector did not feel she could find enough evidence to confirm our 'Good' status for the foreseeable future. In the feedback meeting, she said the official term (not her words, she was at pains to point out) for us now was 'Good but declining'; I had enough spirit left in me to quip "and that's just the Deputy Head", which helped to diffuse a bit of tension in the room, I think. When asked what this meant in practical terms, she explained that we would now face another visit in between twelve- and twenty-four-months' time. This inspection would be graded and could downgrade us if we did not satisfactorily address the concerns identified.

So, another round of Action Planning has kicked in. We have revamped our curriculum planning documents to make the content and the skills being taught crystal clear. We have reviewed our Behaviour Policy and, amongst other things, adopted an online program called 'Class Charts' which allows us to report the behaviour of individual children to their parents on a daily basis. This has proved a lot more workable than some of us at first feared, and it appears to be having a positive effect on concentration in the classroom. I have taken the lead on the curriculum planning side of things and done my best to keep up the energy levels on that even though I know I am leaving, and Elaine, my age but showing no signs of wanting to call it a day, has worked tirelessly on the behaviour initiatives. By the time I retire, sixteen months of the twenty-four-month period will have elapsed, so whether I will have to face the music one final time is not yet clear!

The visit by 'Electric Umbrella' is great. A few children find the music too loud; one or two are okay when given headphones but others prefer to sit quietly in the dining room and read a book. It's a treat to see the adults with learning disabilities interact with our pupils, and to see the children appreciating their efforts.

We've had some superb visitors over the years and they are one of the best. I think back to some of the other really good ones: the environmental campaigner Phil Williams, the footballer and anti-racism advocate Luther Blisset, the author Olaf Falafel. Some have been less successful and lacking in the not inconsiderable skills needed to keep a hall full of children entertained for an hour or so. Monotone voices, dull content, sitting stock still and in the wrong place, or questioning that gets the assembled masses way too excited and impossible to bring back down- we've had all of them. One particularly tortuous visit a few years ago led to my colleague Lisa uttering the immortal line "Where did you find her-inviteaweirdotoschool.com?!" when we were sat in the staffroom trying to get our heads around what we'd just witnessed.

I am now slowly starting to tick off my 'last ever this/ last ever that' list of things. This week is my last ever 'Fun, Fit and Fruity Week.' Last week was my last ever Harvest Festival. As I left the church, Huw teased me with, "well at least we won't have to sing *'Autumn Days'* anymore!" A blessing indeed for some, I'm sure.

Epilogue

Leave it as you Found it.

Friday, November 8th 2024

Today I have been invited to one of the local pubs to accept a final retirement gift- a specially commissioned painting of the school by a local artist who is also an ex-staff member and parent.

I was given a brilliant send off in the summer, which left me feeling very appreciated and valued. Many people worked really hard to make this happen. I was treated to a 'Dress up as Mr Hall Day', two emotional farewell assemblies, a very lively evening barbecue and party, some wonderful farewell gifts and a whole host of kind words.

As it turned out, I did have one final encounter with OFSTED; they visited for two days in the first half of the summer term. When they first phoned, their proposed date clashed with the interviews for my replacement; after a nerve racking few hours, they agreed to defer the inspection. However, we knew that was unlikely to be for long, and, sure enough, a couple of weeks later they were back in touch.

I was desperate for our 'Good' status to be preserved, so that I could at least say that I had left the school in the same state as I had found it. This was to be a two-day inspection with two inspectors carrying it out. I didn't sleep well before either day, and by the second day I was physically present, but functioning only on auto-pilot. The inspectors wanted to see examples of writing being improved after interventions by teachers. Several of my colleagues rushed to provide this evidence, but I'm afraid I shied away from doing so, concerned that my frazzled and ageing brain would do more harm than good. When the feedback came and we learnt that we were indeed getting a 'Good' judgement, I struggled to hold back the tears. All our work on curriculum planning and behaviour had not been in vain.

Now, six months on from the inspection and four from retirement, I am still adjusting to my newfound status but am in no doubt that it was the right decision. I think I got the timing about right; I am pretty sure that I could not have done another year without falling victim to another burnout episode similar to the one I suffered fifteen years ago.

Reflecting on thirty-eight years in the classroom, there are many thoughts that go through my mind as I try and make sense of it all. The overwhelming feeling is one of luck and gratitude. I have been fortunate enough to have thoroughly enjoyed my career- yes at times it's been tough going, but I've worked, almost entirely, with talented and dedicated colleagues and with children who have wanted to learn. It's been extremely rewarding and fulfilling. I'm not a rich man at the end of it all but am comfortably off and should be able to enjoy a pleasant retirement. With the possible exception of the BBC cricket correspondent, I can't really think of anything I'd rather have done. There's an element of pride there too that I stuck at it for so long and that hopefully I've been a positive influence on at least some of my charges.

What about the changes I've seen over my time teaching? I think the expectations and the accountability placed on schools by wider society has increased massively since the mid-80s. I should add, however, that I don't think this is confined to education- you could say the same about most aspects of public life. OFSTED, SATS and so on have brought a lot of added pressure to the job and undoubtedly contributed to some of the recruitment and retention issues that the profession faces. I worry a bit that not enough people will want to do the job in the future, although I was encouraged by the fact that seven people applied to be my successor. Also, I'm concerned teachers are being turned into robots- there's no place anymore for the talented maverick who may not be willing to teach by the book but is a potential inspirer of young minds.

Classrooms have definitely become more inclusive during my career, and that's generally a good thing. Children with a much wider variety of neurodivergent conditions (many of which were not understood forty years ago) are now welcomed into 'mainstream' settings, and as long as this is backed up with adequate funding, it's a win-win situation, both for the neurodivergent pupils and their peers.

What about behaviour? There is little doubt that the smartphone generation have shorter concentration spans, and teachers as a rule probably have to work a bit harder than they did at the start of my career to keep a class onside for a whole lesson. Covid did, I think, have an influence- with some tasks seen as optional during the lockdowns, there are more children now who are reluctant to get on with some pieces of work, but these pupils are still very much in the minority and the average child at Bishop Wood is still as excited to learn about the world as they were a quarter of a century ago.

Technology has been another huge change. When I started, 'Banda Machines' were still the preferred way to create class worksheets; the smell of that Gestetner fluid will never leave me. There were blackboards at the front of every classroom and we wrote on them with chalk, which at times gave me quite bad eczema on my hands. The contrast between that and the 'Google Classroom' era of today is pretty stark.

Back in the pub, I am really pleased with the painting and I mentally check out a few different wall spaces in my house where it could hang. I am delighted and humbled that so many of my ex-colleagues have given up the first couple of hours of their weekend to see the presentation and come and say hello. As the drink flows and some of the old stories are retold, I check in with Debs about the possibility of doing some supply teaching in the not-too-distant future. The golf course, the cricket field, my family, my friends, writing this book- they all have their attractions. But I can't quite give up completely the thrill of teaching just yet.

www.ingramcontent.com/pod-product-compliance
Lightning Source LLC
LaVergne TN
LVHW041223080426

835508LV00011B/1050